Prepare for Grade 6

Second Edition

Summertime Learning

Prepare Your Child for Sixth Grade

Directions in Spanish and English

Editorial Project Manager
Eric Migliaccio

Editor in Chief
Brent L. Fox, M. Ed.

Creative Director
Sarah M. Fournier

Cover Artist
Diem Pascarella

Illustrator
Mark Mason

Art Coordinator
Renée Mc Elwee

Imaging
Amanda R. Harter

Publisher
Mary D. Smith, M.S. Ed.

Teacher Created Resources
12621 Western Avenue
Garden Grove, CA 92841
www.teachercreated.com

ISBN: 978-1-4206-8122-2

Reprinted, 2023 (PO604798)
Made in U.S.A.

Teacher Created Resources

Table of Contents

Table of Contents *(cont.)*

An Important Message

El siguiente es un mensaje importante de la Asociación Nacional de Aprendizaje de Verano.

Estimados padres,

¿Sabían que todos los jóvenes experimentan una pérdida de aprendizaje cuando no participan en actividades educativas durante el verano? Esto significa que parte de lo aprendido durante el año escolar suele evaporarse durante los meses de verano. Sin embargo, la pérdida de aprendizaje se puede prevenir con la ayuda de los padres. El verano es la época ideal para participar en actividades interesantes y divertidas que ayuden a los niños a conservar y desarrollar sus habilidades académicas. Algunas ideas:

- Lean con sus hijos a diario. Visiten juntos la biblioteca local y escojan libros que aborden temas de su interés.
- Pidan a los docentes recomendaciones para la lectura de verano. The Summer Reading List (páginas 92–94 de esta guía) constituye un buen punto de partida.
- Exploren parques, reservas naturales, museos y centros culturales.
- Consideren cada día como un sinfín de posibilidades de aprendizaje. Medir las cantidades en una receta o estudiar un mapa antes de un viaje en auto constituyen algunos modos de adquirir o reforzar una habilidad. Utilicen las Learning Experiences que se encuentran al final de este libro para obtener más ideas.
- Establezcan metas a alcanzar de forma diaria. Por ejemplo, realizar cinco problemas de Matemáticas o leer un capítulo de un libro.
- Alienten a su hijo a completar las actividades de los libros tales como *Summertime Learning*, con el fin de reducir la brecha de aprendizaje que suele producirse en el verano.

Nuestra visión es que cada niño se sienta seguro, saludable y comprometido con el aprendizaje durante el verano. Para obtener más información, diríjanse a *www.summerlearning.org*.

¡Que pasen un verano *memorable*!

Matthew Boulay
NSLA Founder

Using This Book

Como padre, posiblemente sepas que el verano es una época para divertirse. Pero también puede ser un tiempo para aprender y prepararse para el próximo año escolar. Al combinar la diversión con el aprendizaje, los libros incluidos en la serie *Summertime Learning* pueden ayudar a tu hijo a mantenerse en el camino educativo y, a su vez, disfrutar del descanso físico y mental que tanto necesita. Con el fin de ayudarte a ayudarlo, hemos desarrollado un recurso organizado, flexible, práctico y gratificante.

Organizado

Summertime Learning: Prepare Your Child for Sixth Grade se encuentra organizado en torno a un período vacacional de ocho semanas. Incluye dos actividades para cada día de la semana. De lunes a jueves, dichas actividades consisten en una lección de Matemáticas y una lección de lectura o escritura. Los viernes ofrecen un divertido cambio de ritmo e incluyen actividades que se centran en habilidades tales como la creatividad, el pensamiento crítico, la capacidad de seguir instrucciones y la resolución de problemas.

Flexible

Hay muchos modos de utilizar este libro de forma efectiva:

- **Día a día**—Tu hijo puede realizar las actividades en orden, comenzando el primer lunes de las vacaciones. Para cada día de la semana, realizará las dos actividades designadas. (Consulta el calendario de la página 7.)
- **A elección**—Si no quieres que tu hijo realice las actividades estrictamente en el orden en que están presentadas en el libro, puedes elegir una combinación de páginas acorde con sus necesidades e intereses.
- **De todo tipo**—Si sientes que tu hijo necesita más apoyo en un área que en otra, puedes optar por centrarte en las actividades de Matemáticas o Artes del Lenguaje.

Además, las páginas de este libro se encuentran perforadas, lo que permite arrancarlas en caso de ser necesario. Si se escoge este método, se puede decorar una carpeta y designarla especialmente para almacenar las páginas sueltas.

Extra Extra

- Para acceder a un práctico calendario que ayude a establecer expectativas y mantenerse al día, consulta la página 7 de este libro.

- Para incluir más escritura en el programa semanal, consulta los "Journal Topics" en la página 8.
- Para conocer distintos modos de incrementar la lectura de verano y las experiencias de aprendizaje, consulta las páginas 92–96.
- Para páginas de referencia útiles en las áreas de geometría, multiplicación y división, ortografía, revisión y más, lee las páginas 97–103.

Práctico

Los padres desean páginas de actividades que no generen dudas sobre cómo utilizarlas, qué se espera que su hijo haga, y cuáles son las respuestas correctas. Las páginas de *Summertime Learning: Prepare Your Child for Sixth Grade* tienen como objetivo responder a esta necesidad.

En la parte superior de cada página de actividades se ofrecen distintos datos de forma directa y de fácil lectura.

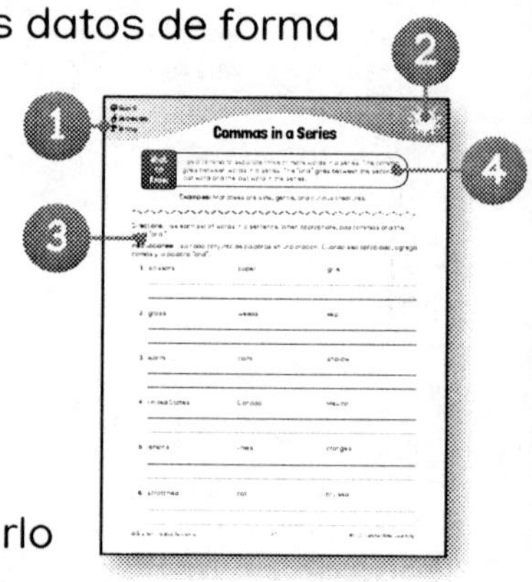

1. En un costado de la página de actividades, se encuentran el día de la semana y el área de aprendizaje. Esto permite a los padres verificar rápidamente en qué se encuentra trabajando su hijo y mantenerse organizados a lo largo del verano.
2. En el costado opuesto de la página figura un ícono de un sol. Constituye el sitio ideal para colocar una calcomanía y, de esta forma, hacer un seguimiento del progreso de tu hijo y recompensarlo cuando completa las actividades incluidas en el libro. Esta función también ayudará a orientarlo hacia las actividades del día siguiente. Al final del libro, encontrarán más de 300 calcomanías coloridas que podrán ser utilizadas para este fin.
3. Las instrucciones para cada una de las actividades se encuentran escritas de forma clara y de un modo que permita comprenderlas fácilmente. Muchas veces sucede que los niños poseen la capacidad de desempeñar una habilidad educativa, pero responden de modo incorrecto porque las instrucciones no son lo suficientemente claras o no han sido leídas en su totalidad.
4. Algunas páginas incluyen un casillero llamado "What to Know" que ofrece un recordatorio de la regla gramatical u ortográfica que tu hijo deberá saber para poder completar la página.

Además, al final del libro se incluye una guía completa de respuestas (páginas 104–111) que puede ser consultada cada vez que se tengan dudas sobre alguna respuesta.

Recompensas

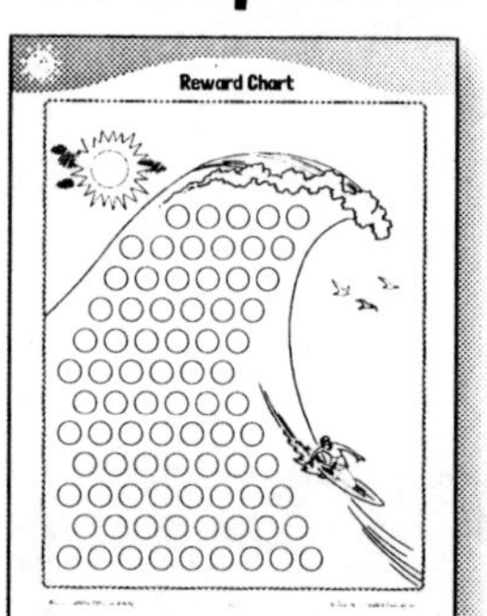

Puedes utilizar el Reward Chart que se encuentra en la página 112 de este libro para realizar un seguimiento de aquellas actividades que ya han sido completadas. Esta página está diseñada para ser utilizada con las calcomanías proporcionadas al final de este libro. Cada vez que tu hijo finalice una página, puede escoger una calcomanía y utilizarla para rellenar uno de los círculos del gráfico.

Las calcomanías también pueden ser utilizadas en las páginas individuales. El sol que se encuentra en la parte superior de la página constituye el sitio ideal para colocar la calcomanía escogida. De este modo, será más fácil orientarlo hacia las actividades del día siguiente: pueden simplemente localizar la última calcomanía colocada y trabajar en las dos páginas consecutivas.

Weekly Calendar

Si lo deseas, puedes utilizar este calendario para planificar el trabajo de tu hijo.

- Cada fila del calendario muestra una semana de aprendizaje. Si te resulta útil, puedes comenzar por añadir las fechas de la semana en la columna de la izquierda.
- Utiliza el renglón que se encuentra bajo cada área de aprendizaje para añadir notas útiles, tales como el número de página donde se encuentra la actividad o el tiempo que le tomó a tu hijo completar cada una de ellas.

Day	Monday	Tuesday	Wednesday	Thursday	Friday
Week 1 __/__/__- __/__/__	☐ Math ☐ Reading	☐ Math ☐ Writing	☐ Math ☐ Reading	☐ Math ☐ Writing	☐ Friday Fun ☐ Friday Fun
Week 2 __/__/__- __/__/__	☐ Math ☐ Writing	☐ Math ☐ Reading	☐ Math ☐ Writing	☐ Math ☐ Reading	☐ Friday Fun ☐ Friday Fun
Week 3 __/__/__- __/__/__	☐ Math ☐ Reading	☐ Math ☐ Writing	☐ Math ☐ Reading	☐ Math ☐ Writing	☐ Friday Fun ☐ Friday Fun
Week 4 __/__/__- __/__/__	☐ Math ☐ Writing	☐ Math ☐ Reading	☐ Math ☐ Writing	☐ Math ☐ Reading	☐ Friday Fun ☐ Friday Fun
Week 5 __/__/__- __/__/__	☐ Math ☐ Reading	☐ Math ☐ Writing	☐ Math ☐ Reading	☐ Math ☐ Writing	☐ Friday Fun ☐ Friday Fun
Week 6 __/__/__- __/__/__	☐ Math ☐ Writing	☐ Math ☐ Reading	☐ Math ☐ Writing	☐ Math ☐ Reading	☐ Friday Fun ☐ Friday Fun
Week 7 __/__/__- __/__/__	☐ Math ☐ Reading	☐ Math ☐ Writing	☐ Math ☐ Reading	☐ Math ☐ Writing	☐ Friday Fun ☐ Friday Fun
Week 8 __/__/__- __/__/__	☐ Math ☐ Writing	☐ Math ☐ Reading	☐ Math ☐ Writing	☐ Math ☐ Reading	☐ Friday Fun ☐ Friday Fun

Journal Topics

Haga que su hijo elija uno de estos temas del diario dos veces por semana. En un diario o cuaderno, pídales que escriban algunas oraciones en respuesta al tema elegido. Recuérdeles que agreguen suficientes detalles para que otra persona que lea sus respuestas sepa lo siguiente sobre su tema:

Quién   Qué   Cuándo   Donde   Por qué   Cómo

Si lo deseas, puedes utilizar lo siguiente como herramienta de organización. Marca la fecha en que tu hijo completó cada consigna.

#1 the best sport or game to play with my friends Completed: ______	#2 the country I most want to know more about Completed: ______	#3 the afterschool job I would most want to have Completed: ______
#4 the best snack food ever created Completed: ______	#5 the skill I could best teach someone how to do Completed: ______	#6 the type of music I most enjoy Completed: ______
#7 the best way to improve the mental or physical health of kids my age Completed: ______	#8 the reasons why students should/shouldn't have cell phones at school Completed: ______	#9 the best thing about a rainy day Completed: ______
#10 the best way to enjoy ice cream Completed: ______	#11 the best type of pet to have Completed: ______	#12 the type of business I would most want to own one day Completed: ______
#13 the reasons why sleeping in a tent is/isn't preferable to sleeping in a hotel Completed: ______	#14 the place I would most want to build my future home Completed: ______	#15 the things I can do to improve the world for those younger than me Completed: ______
#16 the reasons I would/wouldn't want to be a doctor Completed: ______	#17 the best item I have bought with my own money Completed: ______	#18 the most regrettable item I have bought with my own money Completed: ______

Standards and Skills

Estándares Educativos

Cada una de las actividades incluidas en *Summertime Learning: Prepare Your Child for Sixth Grade* cumple con uno o más de los estándares educativos nacionales. Para conocer cómo se relacionan específicamente las actividades con los estándares básicos estatales, visita *http://www.teachercreated.com/standards.*

- Desplázate hacia abajo en la lista alfabética para encontrar la *Summertime Learning (2nd Edition)* series.
- Haz clic en **Standards** el link para acceder a TCR8846 Summertime Learning Grade 6 Standards.

Habilidades Introducidas y Reforzadas

Las actividades de *Summertime Learning: Prepare Your Child for Sixth Grade* tienen como objetivo reforzar las habilidades aprendidas en el quinto grado, así como introducir otras nuevas que luego serán desarrolladas en el sexto grado. Dichas habilidades se encuentran enumeradas a continuación, y en la página 10–11.

Escritura

- Escribe un texto expositivo
- Escribe en respuesta a una experiencia personal
- Escribe en respuesta a la literatura
- Utiliza estrategias para redactar trabajos escritos
- Utiliza estrategias para corregir y revisar trabajos escritos
- Utiliza la forma de párrafo en el trabajo escrito
- Utiliza un lenguaje descriptivo para mejorar las ideas
- Utiliza varias partes del discurso: sustantivos, verbos, adjetivos, adverbios, pronombres, preposiciones, etc.—en trabajos escritos
- Escribe un contenido que sea apropiado para una audiencia específica y propósitos específicos
- Utiliza un estilo apropiado para audiencias y propósitos específicos
- Escribe usando una variedad de géneros
- Utiliza las convenciones de la gramática en el trabajo escrito
- Muestra comprensión de la ortografía en el trabajo escrito
- Muestra comprensión de las mayúsculas en el trabajo escrito
- Muestra comprensión de la puntuación en el trabajo escrito

Standards and Skills *(cont.)*

Habilidades Introducidas y Reforzadas *(cont.)*

Lectura

- Entiende y ajusta los propósitos para la lectura
- Entiende el vocabulario de lectura apropiado para el grado
- Utiliza estrategias para mejorar el vocabulario de la lectura
- Lee una variedad de pasajes y textos literarios
- Lee una variedad de géneros literarios
- Conoce las características que definan varios géneros literarios
- Comprende los elementos de la trama y el desarrollo de los personajes
- Entiende el uso de dispositivos literarios específicos
- Entiende los propósitos y usos del punto de vista
- Hace conexiones entre los personajes y el desarrollo de la trama en un texto y aquellos en tu propia vida
- Resume y parafrasea información en textos
- Utiliza nueva información para ajustar y ampliar la comprensión personal
- Saca conclusiones y hace inferencias basadas en la información explícita e implícita en textos

Matemática

- Utiliza una variedad de estrategias para resolver problemas
- Entiende que los diferentes métodos de resolución de problemas tienen ventajas y desventajas
- Determina la información requerida para resolver un problema y elige métodos para obtener esa información
- Entiende que los símbolos escritos representan ideas matemáticas
- Suma, resta, multiplica y divide números enteros y otros números racionales
- Suma y resta fracciones con distinto denominador
- Multiplica y divide fracciones
- Comprende el orden correcto de las operaciones para resolver cálculos matemáticos

Habilidades Introducidas y Reforzadas *(cont.)*

Matemática *(cont.)*

- Comprende el rol de los números enteros positivos y negativos en el sistema numérico
- Comprende las propiedades de las operaciones con números racionales
- Entiende cómo se puede usar la matemática para resolver problemas del mundo real
- Entiende las características y usos de los exponentes
- Comprende las características y usos de la notación científica
- Comprende los conceptos de razones, proporciones y porcentajes
- Entiende cómo se pueden usar fórmulas para encontrar medidas
- Resuelve problemas que tengan perímetros o áreas de varias formas
- Entiende que las medidas lineales se registran en unidades
- Entiende que las medidas de área se registran en unidades cuadradas
- Entiende que las medidas de volumen se registran en unidades cúbicas
- Comprende las propiedades definitorias de las figuras bidimensionales y tridimensionales
- Entiende cómo leer los datos representados en varios cuadros, tablas y gráficos
- Entiende cómo aplicar datos para crear varios cuadros, tablas y gráficos
- Entiende cómo determinar la probabilidad
- Entiende cómo encontrar promedios cuando se le da un conjunto de números
- Entiende cómo las predicciones pueden basarse en datos y probabilidades
- Entiende operaciones básicas en operaciones algebraicas

Add Three Numbers

Directions: Solve each problem. Write each sum in the number puzzle.

Instrucciones: Resuelve cada problema. Escribe cada una de las sumas en el rompecabezas de números.

Across

2. 713 + 595 + 664

3. 184 + 432 + 629

4. 711 + 490 + 528

5. 572 + 444 + 783

6. 881 + 357 + 795

7. 751 + 953 + 642

8. 487 + 507 + 109

10. 512 + 579 + 830

11. 314 + 973 + 818

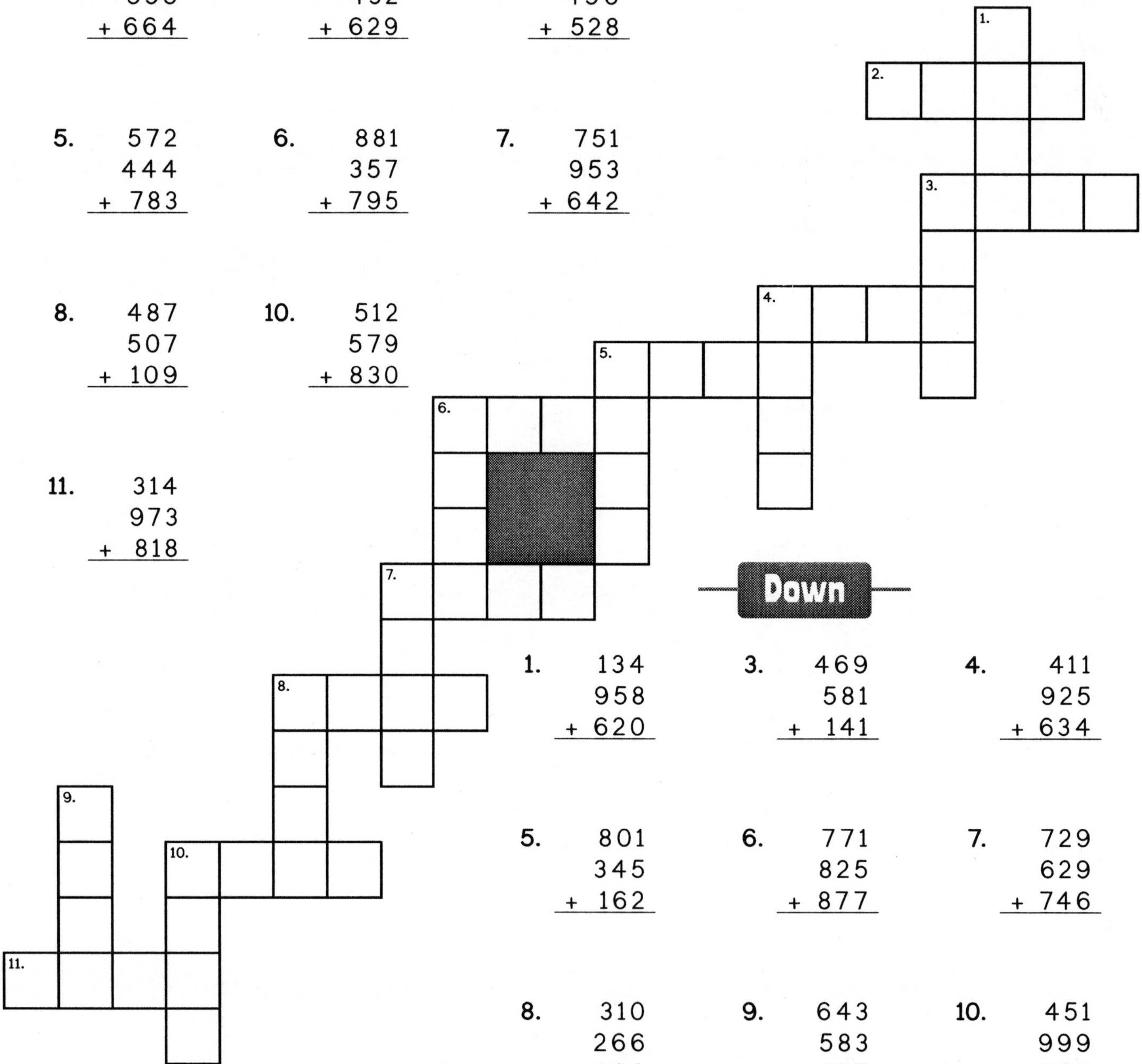

Down

1. 134 + 958 + 620

3. 469 + 581 + 141

4. 411 + 925 + 634

5. 801 + 345 + 162

6. 771 + 825 + 877

7. 729 + 629 + 746

8. 310 + 266 + 466

9. 643 + 583 + 185

10. 451 + 999 + 308

The Aztecs

Directions: Read the passage, then circle the correct answers below.

Instrucciones: Lee el párrafo, luego haz un círculo alrededor de las respuestas correctas.

The Aztecs were the last people to settle in the Valley of Mexico, high in the volcanic mountains of central Mexico. There, on the shores of shallow, marshy Lake Tezcoco, they built an impressive center for their empire.

The Aztecs were a semi-nomadic tribe of Chichimecs who arrived in the Valley of Mexico about 1200 CE. According to oral traditions and codices (ancient manuscripts), the ancestral home of the Aztecs was Aztlan, a place northwest of Mexico City. No one has identified an exact location. Legend has it that about 1100 CE, the god Huizilopochtli (Blue Hummingbird) instructed them to wander until they found an eagle on a cactus eating a snake. There they would build their capital.

After many stops and skirmishes, they settled on the west side of Tezcoco, at a place called Chapultapec (Grasshopper Hill). Other tribes drove the Aztecs out, but the Colhua allowed the Aztecs to live near them in exchange for the services of Aztec soldiers. Finally tired of being under the Colhuacans, the Aztecs killed the daughter of the ruler and then fled into the marshy lake. On one island, they saw an eagle on a cactus. At the site of this sign, the Aztecs built their capital, Tenochtitlán.

In the 200 years from the sighting of the eagle (about 1325 CE) to the arrival of the Spanish (1521 CE), the Aztecs grew to be the most powerful people in the Valley of Mexico. They adopted many elements from the cultures that had preceded them and built one of the most impressive cities of Mesoamerica.

1. Based on the passage, how do you think people first learned about the Aztecs?
   - a. reading textbooks
   - b. oral traditions and codices
   - c. in the newspaper
   - d. on the Internet

2. What does *Huizilopochtli* mean?
   - a. Valley of Mexico
   - b. Blue Hummingbird
   - c. Grasshopper Hill
   - d. capital city

3. The Aztec capital was named
   - a. Aztlan.
   - b. Tezcoco.
   - c. Tenochtitlán.
   - d. Mesoamerica.

4. What sign did the Aztecs look for to know where to build their capital?
   - a. an eagle on a cactus
   - b. a fish in the lake
   - c. lightning hitting the mountain
   - d. a blue hummingbird

Supplies Multiplied

Directions: Use the chart to solve each problem below. Circle your final answers. The first one has been done for you.

Instrucciones: Usa la tabla para resolver cada problema. Encierra en un círculo a tus respuestas finales. El primero ha sido hecho para ti.

Supply Room Inventory

pencils 68 per box	erasers 847 per box	crayons 271 per box	markers 199 per box
rulers 952 per box	notepads 88 per box	hole punchers 348 per box	binders 17 per box
pens 1,107 per box	rubber bands 75 per box	sheets of paper 6,050 per box	folders 1,104 per box

1. 61 boxes of rulers 952 × 61 952 + 57,120 58,072	2. 27 boxes of pencils	3. 71 boxes of binders	4. 92 boxes of erasers
5. 373 boxes of notepads	6. 29 boxes of pens	7. 113 boxes of rubber bands	8. 314 boxes of hole punchers
9. 164 boxes of paper	10. 217 boxes of markers	11. 73 boxes of crayons	12. 89 boxes of folders

Sensory Words

What to Know **Sensory words** are words that describe how something feels, looks, sounds, smells, or tastes.

Directions: Write a sentence that uses one of the five senses to describe a given word. Circle the word that describes how the object feels, looks, sounds, smells, or tastes. Then, write the sense you used. An example has been done for you.

Instrucciones: Escribe una oración que use uno de los cinco sentidos para describir una palabra dada. Haz un círculo alrededor de la palabra que describa cómo se siente, se ve, suena, huele o sabe. Luego, escribe el sentido que usaste. Un ejemplo ha sido hecho para ti.

Object	Your Sentence	Sense Used
1. soccer ball	I wiped off the (dusty) soccer ball.	sight
2. lemon		
3. trashcan		
4. snake		
5. pizza		
6. shoes		
7. cactus		
8. alarm clock		

Divide and Multiply

Directions: Write the division problem and solve. Multiply to check the answer. The first one has been done for you.

Instrucciones: Escribe el problema de división y resuelve. Multiplica para comprobar la respuesta. El ejemplo es para ti.

1. 8,400 cookies divided into 40 boxes Solve: 40)8400 = 210 -80 40 -40 00 Check: 210 × 40 000 +8,400 8,400	2. 41,796 pieces of bubble gum divided into 172 cartons Solve Check	3. 33,320 decks of playing cards divided into 136 cases Solve Check
4. 3,822 marbles placed into 91 pouches Solve Check	5. 8,928 potato chips placed into 9 gigantic bowls Solve Check	6. 28,917 game pieces for 81 board games Solve Check
7. 35,620 paper clips placed into 260 canisters Solve Check	8. 180,930 ants in 37 colonies Solve Check	9. 8,840 peanuts for 65 elephants Solve Check

Mexico's Past

Directions: Read the passage, then circle the correct answers below.

Instrucciones: Lee el párrafo, luego haz encierra las respuestas correctas a continuación.

Hundreds of years ago, American Indian tribes lived in Mexico. The Aztecs built beautiful cities. They had a calendar and a written language. However, the Spanish destroyed the Aztecs in 1521. For the next 300 years, Spain ruled over Mexico. This is why the language of Mexico is Spanish.

Every September 16, the Mexican people hold a celebration in Mexico City, their country's capital. It is their Independence Day. On that date in 1821, they told Spain they would no longer be ruled. Breaking free from Spain caused a war. When it was over, the Mexicans had their own government. They made their own laws.

Today, America and Mexico are friends, but it wasn't always that way. President James Polk wanted America to reach from the Atlantic Ocean to the Pacific Ocean. He tried to buy what is now the American Southwest from Mexico. Mexico would not sell. So from 1846 to 1848, Mexico and America fought a war to **ascertain** where their borders would be. When the war ended, Mexico had lost a lot of land. Now the Rio Grande River forms the border between the two nations. America is on the north side of the river. Mexico is on the south side.

1. U.S. President James Polk wanted
   a. the U.S. to expand its borders.
   b. Mexico to change its Independence Day to July 4th.
   c. the country of Mexico to become one of the states of the Union.
   d. Americans to adopt the Mexican language.
2. According to the passage, what happened second?
   a. Mexicans declared their independence from Spain.
   b. The Spanish ruled over Mexico.
   c. The Aztecs built cities in Mexico.
   d. Americans fought a war with Mexico.
3. Another word for *ascertain* is
   a. inspect. b. change. c. battle. d. determine.
4. Before the Aztecs were conquered, they probably
   a. didn't speak Spanish.
   b. couldn't read or write any language.
   c. didn't have any tools.
   d. didn't understand the concept of time.

Multiplying Decimals

Directions: Multiply to solve each problem. Show your work.

Instrucciones: Multiplica para resolver cada problema. Muestra tu trabajo.

Keys to Multiplying Decimals

- Line up the numbers. However, you don't need to line up the decimal points.
- Multiply the numbers as you would multiply whole numbers.
- Count the number of decimal places in both numbers that are being multiplied. Make sure the decimal places in the product equal the number of decimal places in the problem.

1. \$44.88 × 2	2. \$4.49 × 3	3. \$21.06 × 5
4. \$19.99 × 7	5. \$1.57 × 34	6. \$105.13 × 4
7. \$37.03 × 13	8. \$17.10 × 15	9. 0.84 × 3.15
10. 2.08 × 0.9	11. 0.28 × 9.51	12. 0.0076 × 0.30
13. \$10.50 × 0.60	14. 47.8 × 0.1	15. 14.2 × 9.7

Analogies

What to Know

- **Antonyms** are words that are opposite in meaning.
- **Synonyms** are words that mean the same.
- An **analogy** is a comparison of two things based on their being alike in some way.

Directions: Choose the answer that best completes the analogy. Write **synonyms** or **antonyms** on the blank line to describe the relationship between the words in each pair. The first one is done for you.

Instrucciones: Elige la respuesta que mejor complete la analogía. Escribe **synonyms** o **antonyms** en la línea en blanco para describir la relación entre las palabras de cada par. Un ejemplo ha sido hecho para ti.

1. marvelous : great Ⓐ drenched : wet (filled in) Ⓑ silly : serious Ⓒ dull : exciting Ⓓ gorgeous : ugly synonyms	2. rapid : slow Ⓐ wait : remain Ⓑ shrink : increase Ⓒ stare : peer Ⓓ stop : cease __________	3. err : correct Ⓐ teach : educate Ⓑ muffle : silence Ⓒ aid : hinder Ⓓ shout : yell __________
4. rival : competitor Ⓐ teacher : student Ⓑ doctor : patient Ⓒ pilot : airplane Ⓓ jester : clown __________	5. spry : stiff Ⓐ lucky : fortunate Ⓑ tardy : early Ⓒ tender : caring Ⓓ normal : average __________	6. confuse : bewilder Ⓐ squeeze : expand Ⓑ employ : hire Ⓒ squabble : agree Ⓓ mistreat : help __________
7. monitor : watch Ⓐ steal : return Ⓑ lead : follow Ⓒ fracture : break Ⓓ plant : uproot __________	8. harsh : tender Ⓐ lush : barren Ⓑ lazy : sluggish Ⓒ happy : cheerful Ⓓ lean : slender __________	9. flicker : blink Ⓐ insist : demand Ⓑ relax : toil Ⓒ tighten : loosen Ⓓ stumble : leap __________

Map Madness!

Do you see Juanita? She is lost! Follow the directions to get her back on track. Mark her ending spot with an X. Use the compass rose to help you.

¿Ves a Juanita? ¡Ella está perdida! Sigue las instrucciones para que vuelva al camino. Marca su punto final con una X. Usa la rosa de los vientos para ayudarte.

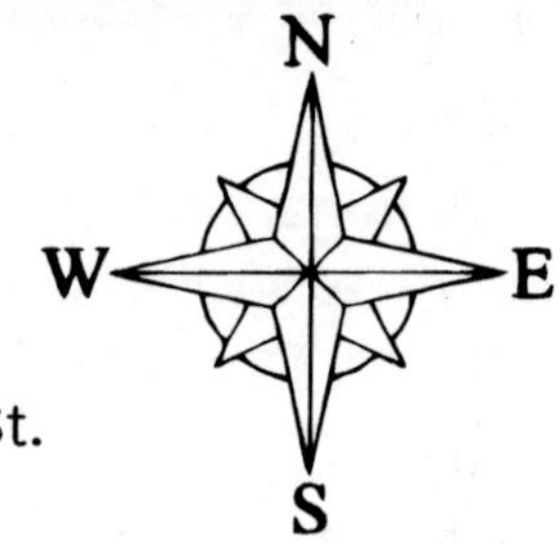

Directions:

1. Go north on 2nd Ave.
2. Head east on Union St.
3. Go south on 5th Ave.
4. Go east on Spring St.
5. Head south on 7th Ave.
6. END Go 3 blocks and stop.

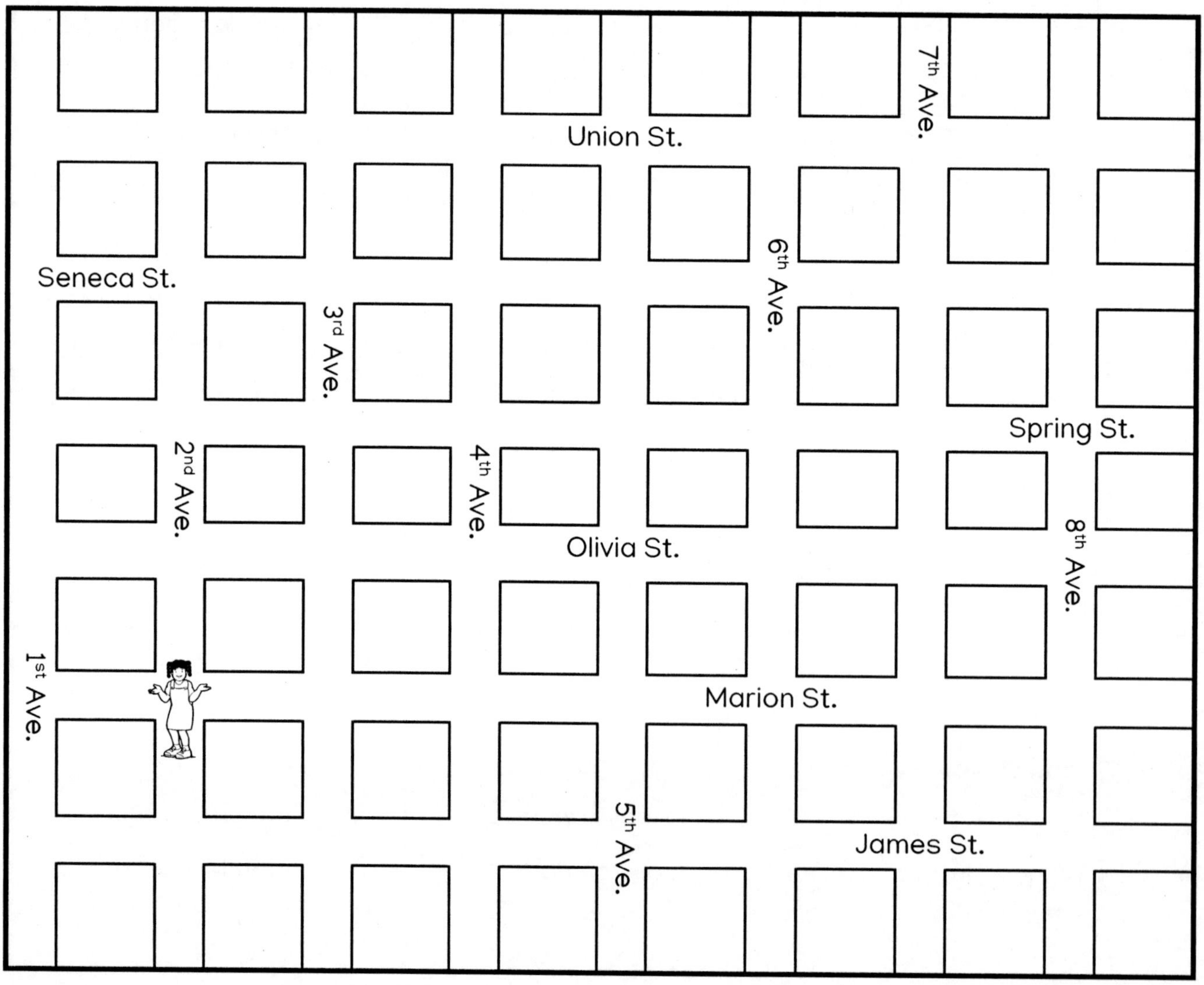

Obscured Animals

Directions: If something is *obscured*, it is not easily seen. It is hidden. In the sentences below, the names of animals are hidden. And to add to the challenge, these animals are a bit more obscure. (Obscure can also mean "not as well known.") So don't look for *dog* or *cat* or *cow*! But do use the number of letters in parentheses as a clue to help you find each answer. (And if you need a little more help, check out the "Bonus Hints" at the bottom of the page.)

Instrucciones: Si algo está *oscurecido*, no se ve fácilmente. Está escondido. En las oraciones, los nombres de los animales están escondidos. Y para agregar al desafío, estos animales son un poco más oscuros. (Oscuro también puede significar "no tan conocido"). ¡Así que no busques *perros*, *gatos* o *vacas*! Pero usa el número de letras entre paréntesis como clave para ayudarte a encontrar cada respuesta. (Y si necesitas un poco más de ayuda, consulta los "Bonus Hints" en la parte inferior de la página).

1. Jim was painting a picture. (4) wasp
2. You scratched the car I bought yesterday! (7) ____________
3. Mary took a picture of the pretty sunset. (5) ____________
4. The magician's tricks are all amazing. (5) ____________
5. Aren't these toys terrific? (6) ____________
6. Grandma gave a gleeful smile when she saw us. (5) ____________
7. The golfer retired after sinking his final shot. (6) ____________
8. From the shadows, the ninja guarded the gate. (6) ____________
9. The hungry man ate eight pepperoni pizzas! (7) ____________
10. She handled the whole fiasco bravely. (5) ____________

Bonus Hints: The animals hidden in problems 2, 3, 4, 7, 8, and 9 are mammals. The animal hidden in 5 is a mollusk. The animal in 6 is a bird. The one in 10 is a reptile.

Converting Temperature

Directions: Use the formulas in the box below to convert each temperature. Write each temperature to the hundredths place without rounding and complete the number puzzle. Be sure to include the decimal points in the puzzle.

Instrucciones: Usa las fórmulas en el cuadro para convertir cada temperatura. Escribe cada temperatura en centésimas de las centésimas sin redondear y completa el acertijo numérico. Asegúrate de incluir los puntos decimales en el rompecabezas.

Formulas	
	°F to °C: subtract 32°, then divide by 1.8
	°C to °F: multiply by 1.8, then add 32°

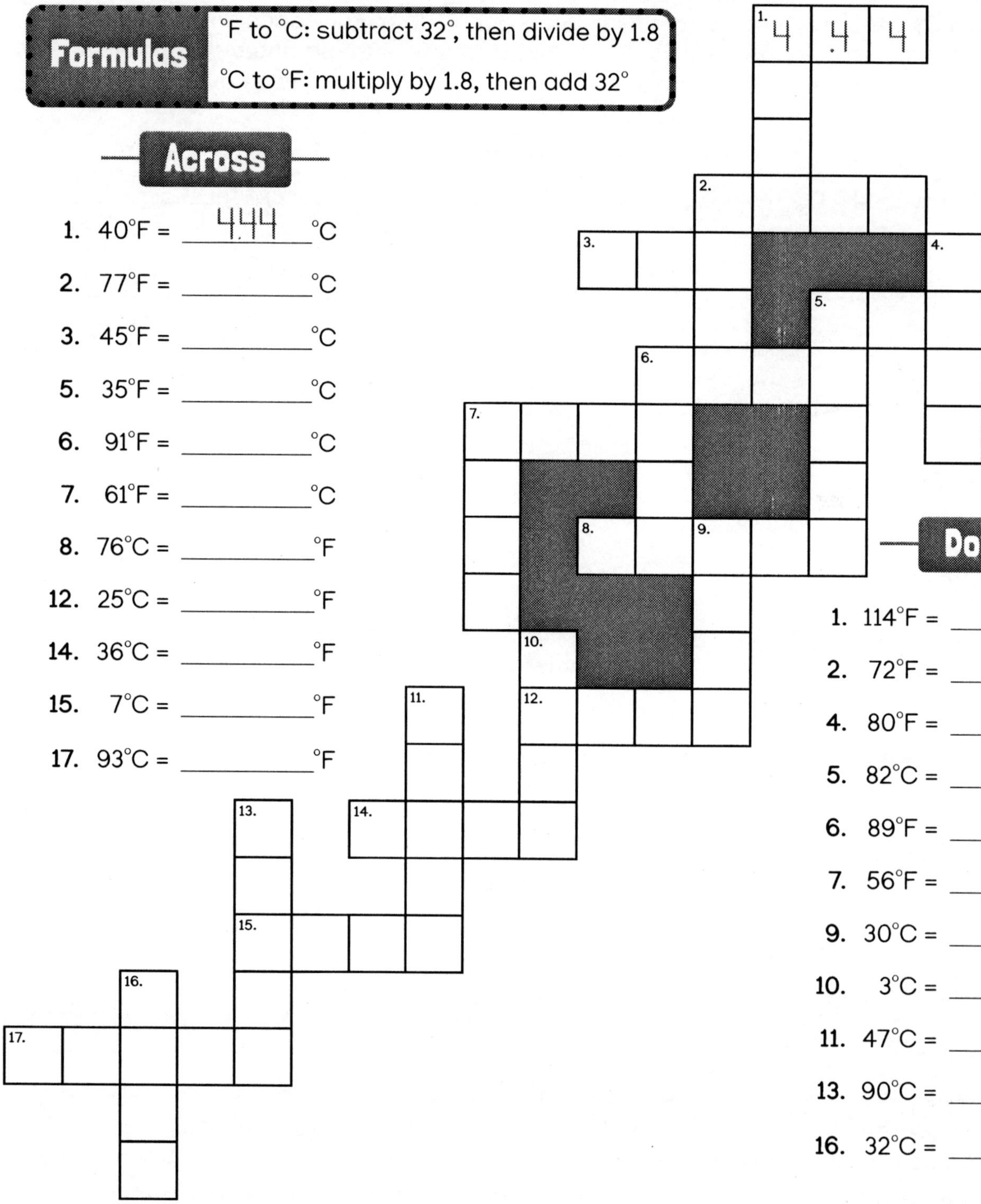

Across

1. 40°F = 4.44 °C
2. 77°F = ________ °C
3. 45°F = ________ °C
5. 35°F = ________ °C
6. 91°F = ________ °C
7. 61°F = ________ °C
8. 76°C = ________ °F
12. 25°C = ________ °F
14. 36°C = ________ °F
15. 7°C = ________ °F
17. 93°C = ________ °F

Down

1. 114°F = ________ °C
2. 72°F = ________ °C
4. 80°F = ________ °C
5. 82°C = ________ °F
6. 89°F = ________ °C
7. 56°F = ________ °C
9. 30°C = ________ °F
10. 3°C = ________ °F
11. 47°C = ________ °F
13. 90°C = ________ °F
16. 32°C = ________ °F

Antonym Crossword

Directions: Fill in the crossword puzzle with the antonyms of the words below. *Hint:* All of the answers start with "C" or "D." A few answers have been done for you.

Instrucciones: Completa el crucigrama con los antónimos de las siguientes palabras. *Clave*: Todas las respuestas comienzan con "C" o "D". Hay ejemplos para ti.

Across

The antonym of . . .

3. rare
4. pick up
8. avoid
9. destroy
10. cheerful
11. contrast
12. alive
13. open
14. hot
17. laughed

Down

The antonym of . . .

1. robber
2. incorrect
3. original
5. cloudless
6. uncovered
7. unimportant
11. straight
12. shallow
13. sane
15. night
16. light

Time Change

Directions: Complete the chart by converting hours into minutes and seconds.

Instrucciones: Completa el cuadro convirtiendo horas en minutos y segundos.

	Hours	Minutes	Seconds
1.	$\frac{1}{4}$		
2.	$\frac{1}{2}$		
3.	$\frac{3}{4}$		
4.	1		
5.	2		
6.	3		
7.	4		
8.	6		
9.	8		
10.	12		
11.	18		
12.	24		

Directions: Use the < or > symbols to compare each pair of times.

Instrucciones: Usa los símbolos < o > para comparar las horas.

13.	210 seconds ◯ 2 minutes	**14.**	98 minutes ◯ 2 hours
15.	27 minutes ◯ 630 seconds	**16.**	4 hours ◯ 16,641 seconds

Mummies

Directions: Read the passage, then circle the correct answers.

Instrucciones: Lee el párrafo, luego encierra las respuestas correctas.

Thousands of years ago, people in Ancient Egypt thought that dead people needed their bodies after death. They believed that the people continued to live in a place called the afterlife, so they found a way to keep dead bodies from rotting. They figured out how to turn dead people into mummies. They **preserved** most of their kings and queens this way.

It was a lot of work to make a mummy. First, priests washed the dead body. Then, they removed all of the organs—even the brain! They put a kind of salt all over the body. After six weeks, the body completely dried out. Next, they stuffed the body with sand, sawdust, or cloth. This made the body look full again. Then, they rubbed spices and oils into the skin. Finally, the priests wrapped cloth strips tightly around each part of the body. Wrapping the body took about two weeks. Lastly, they put the body into a coffin. On its cover, the coffin had paintings and sometimes gems.

The most famous mummy is King Tut. He was still a teenager when he died over 4,000 years ago. He was put into a secret tomb. Scientists found this tomb in 1922. His family had put all sorts of gold, gems, and other riches into his tomb. Inside, King Tut's mummy lay in a solid gold coffin. Even his sandals were made of solid gold.

1. Ancient Egyptians believed dead kings and queens
   - a. would use their belongings after they died.
   - b. should be burned instead of buried.
   - c. would send good luck to their people.
   - d. would return to their throne after they died.

2. What did the priests do last when making a mummy?
   - a. They washed the body.
   - b. They removed the organs.
   - c. They wrapped the body.
   - d. They stuffed the body.

3. Egyptians mummified their rulers because
   - a. they thought it would make the rulers look better in the afterlife.
   - b. they believed the rulers needed their bodies in the afterlife.
   - c. they wanted to use the rulers' organs.
   - d. they hoped the rulers would be found years later.

4. The opposite of *preserved* is
   - a. kept.
   - b. worshipped.
   - c. ruined.
   - d. changed.

Dividing Decimals

What to Know

If the divisor has a decimal, move it to the right of the divisor. Then, move the decimal in the dividend the same number of places to the right. If there are not enough spaces to the right in the dividend, add zeroes until there are enough spaces.

Example: divisor → .12)24.36 ← dividend

Step 1: Move the decimal to the right of the divisor. 12.)24.36

Step 2: Move the decimal in the dividend the same number of places to the right. 12.)2436.

Step 3: Solve.

```
        203
12. )2436.
      24
       03
      - 0
       036
      - 36
         0
```

Directions: Solve the division problems. Round to the nearest hundredth when needed. Use another sheet of paper to show your work.

Instrucciones: Resuelve los problemas de división. Redondea a la centésima más cercana cuando sea necesario. Utiliza otra hoja de papel para mostrar su trabajo.

1. .14) .7	2. .6) 43.2	3. 9.2) 230
4. .04) 30	5. .24) 42	6. 0.8) 65
7. .34) 93.8	8. 5.1) 13.61	9. 9.17) .356

Multiple Meanings

What to Know

Many words from daily conversation and writing can be used in a variety of ways. One example is the word *quarter*:

- Avery saves all his *quarters* in his largest piggy bank. *(noun)*
- A *quarter* portion of the pizza was given to each person. *(adjective)*
- *Quarter* the apple pie so that we can all have a piece. *(verb)*

Directions: For each word, write two sentences. In each sentence, use a different definition of the word.

Instrucciones: Por cada palabra, escribe dos oraciones. En cada oración, usa una definición distinta de la palabra.

1. **fast**

   a. ______________________________

   b. ______________________________

2. **side**

   a. ______________________________

   b. ______________________________

3. **number**

   a. ______________________________

   b. ______________________________

4. **good**

   a. ______________________________

   b. ______________________________

5. **just**

   a. ______________________________

   b. ______________________________

6. **retreat**

   a. ______________________________

   b. ______________________________

Car Calculations

Directions: Use your knowledge of decimal operations to compare the results for each car tested. Show your work on a separate sheet of paper.

Instrucciones: Use su conocimiento de las operaciones decimales para comparar los resultados de cada coche probado. Muestra tu trabajo en una hoja de papel por separado.

Question	Answer
1. A station wagon traveled 248.9 miles on a tank of gas. A sedan traveled 218.576 miles on a tank of gas. How far did they travel altogether?	
2. A hybrid car is powered by a combination of electrical batteries and gasoline. This vehicle traveled 112.34 miles on one gallon of gasoline. How many miles would it travel on 20 gallons of gasoline?	
3. The stopping distance for the Laser Racer was 45.678 feet. The stopping distance for the Super Sport was 78.1 feet. What is the difference?	
4. A regular gasoline-powered car traveled exactly 18.2 miles on a gallon of gasoline. The hybrid car went 112.34 miles on a gallon of gas. How much farther did the hybrid car travel on one gallon?	
5. The New Wave Motor Company has developed an SUV that travels 580.75 miles on 25 gallons of gasoline. How far can it travel on 1 gallon of gasoline?	
6. A sports car traveled 198.764 miles on one tank of gas. A sedan traveled 243.4 miles on one tank of gas. How much farther did the sedan travel?	
7. The maximum speed of a battery-powered vehicle was 172.387 miles per hour. The maximum speed of a gasoline-powered roadster was 220.2 miles per hour. How much faster was the roadster?	
8. A classic car from the 1960s weighs 4,173.96 pounds. A battery-powered experimental vehicle weighs 1,143.003 pounds. How much heavier is the classic car?	
9. An experimental car traveled 819.45 miles on 9 gallons of gas. How far did it travel on 1 gallon of gas?	
10. An experimental motorcycle can travel 189.34 miles on a gallon of gas. How far could it travel on a full tank holding 4.65 gallons of gas?	

Army Underground

Directions: Read the passage, then circle the correct answers.

Instrucciones: Lee el párrafo, luego haz un círculo alrededor de las respuestas correctas.

Qin Shi Huangdi was a great Chinese emperor. He was the first emperor of the Qin dynasty. A dynasty is a series of rulers from the same family. The Qin dynasty began over 2,200 years ago when Qin unified several small states. Qin unified the states under a strong central government.

Qin is famous for a wall. The wall is known as the Great Wall of China. The Great Wall of China is over 2,000 miles long. Qin built it to protect the country against intruders. An **intruder** is one who forces himself or herself upon others. The Great Wall is high and wide. It is the longest man-made structure on Earth.

Qin is also famous for an army. The army is made up of over 7,500 warriors. Some of the warriors stand at attention. Other warriors, such as the archers, kneel. These warriors are armed with spears, bows, and arrows. Other armed warriors are on horses. Qin's army can still be seen today. One can understand how Qin's wall can still be seen today, but how is it possible to view Qin's army?

In 1974, two farmers were digging a well in central China. When their hole was about 14 feet deep, their shovels hit something hard. They thought it was a terra-cotta pot. Terra-cotta pots are dull brownish-red. They are made of clay. As the farmers dug further, they were shocked at what they found. Instead of a pot, they found a head! They were even more astounded when they found the head was attached to a body!

Archaeologists were called in. Archaeologists study ancient times and ancient peoples. The archaeologists were astounded at the find. The terra-cotta warrior was life-size. His face was perfectly sculpted, or formed. As the archaeologists continued to dig, they found an entire life-size army standing in formation 20 feet below the ground. Each warrior had a perfectly sculpted head, no two of which were the same. Each warrior had real weapons. Qin built the terra-cotta army to protect his tomb!

1. This story is mainly about
   a. what Qin did.
   b. ancient China.
   c. the Great Wall.
   d. what archaeologists found.

2. Qin's army is made up of over
   a. 20 warriors.
   b. 2,200 warriors.
   c. 7,500 warriors.
   d. 75,200 warriors.

3. One can view Qin's army today because
   a. it is life-size.
   b. it has been uncovered.
   c. Qin ruled over 2,200 years ago.
   d. it was built to protect Qin's tomb.

4. Think about how the word *intruder* relates to *guest*. What words relate in the same way?
   a. ancient : old
   b. terra-cotta : clay
   c. unified : separate
   d. surprised : astounded

Words Add Up

Directions: In the Points Box, each letter has been given a point value. The total point value of a word can be found by adding the point values of all the letters in the word. For example, the value of the word *be* would be 7. (*b* = 2 points and *e* = 5 points, so 2 + 5 = 7)

Instrucciones: En el "Points Box", a cada letra se le ha asignado un valor en puntos. El valor total en puntos de una palabra se puede encontrar sumando los valores en puntos de todas las letras en la palabra. Por ejemplo, el valor de la palabra "be" sería 7. (*b* = 2 puntos y *e* = 5 puntos, entonces 2 + 5 = 7)

Points Box
a = 1
b = 2
c = 3
d = 4
e = 5
f = 6
g = 7
h = 8
i = 9
j = 10
k = 11
l = 12
m = 13
n = 14
o = 15
p = 16
q = 17
r = 18
s = 19
t = 20
u = 21
v = 22
w = 23
x = 24
y = 25
z = 26

For problems #1–#3, guess which word would have a higher point value. Write your guess. Then, do the math to determine if you were correct.

1. puppy kitten **Your Guess:** ____________

   Actual Values: puppy ________ kitten ________

2. igloo house **Your Guess:** ____________

   Actual Values: igloo ________ house ________

3. pizza sandwich **Your Guess:** ____________

   Actual Values: pizza ________ sandwich ________

Directions: Now see if you can make words that fit the following rules. Show your math. Do not use a word from the section above.

Instrucciones: Ahora ve si puedes formar palabras que se ajusten a las siguientes reglas. Muestra tu matemática. No uses una palabra de la sección anterior.

4. a word with 6 letters or fewer that is worth 80 points or more

   Word: ____________________

   Equation: ____ = ____________

5. a word with 8 letters or fewer that is worth 100 points or more

   Word: ____________________

   Equation: ____ = ____________

Name that Team

Directions: Find the name of the football, basketball, baseball, or hockey team that fits each clue. Choose your answer from the Team List.

Instrucciones: Encuentre el nombre del equipo de fútbol, baloncesto, béisbol o hockey que se ajuste a cada clave. Elige tu respuesta de la "Team List".

Team List				
Broncos	Diamondbacks	Jazz	Lions	Padres
Clippers	Dolphins	Kings	Marlins	Pistons
Colts	Eagles	Lightning	Nets	

1. tools used to help fishermen ____________________
2. fathers ____________________
3. aquatic mammals ____________________
4. young horses ____________________
5. endangered birds ____________________
6. kings of the jungle ____________________
7. parts of a car ____________________
8. big fish ____________________
9. style of music ____________________
10. queens' spouses ____________________
11. scissors ____________________
12. wild horses ____________________
13. venomous snakes ____________________
14. bolt of electricity ____________________

Exponents Crossword

Directions: Calculate the answer to each problem. Write each answer in the number puzzle. Remember, the exponent tells the number of times to multiply the base by itself.

Instrucciones: Calcula la respuesta para cada problema. Escribe cada respuesta en el rompecabezas de números. Recuerda, el exponente te dice el número de veces que hay que multiplicar la base por sí misma.

Across

2. 7^5 = 7 × 7 × 7 × 7 × 7 = 16,807
3. 5^3 = ____________
5. 11^3 = ____________
10. 9^6 = ____________
12. 7^2 = ____________
13. 4^4 = ____________
14. 5^4 = ____________
16. 12^2 = ____________
17. 11^4 = ____________
19. 2^4 = ____________

Down

1. 10^3 = ____________
2. 5^6 = ____________
4. 3^5 = ____________
6. 7^3 = ____________
7. 8^4 = ____________
8. 5^5 = ____________
9. 9^4 = ____________
11. 4^5 = ____________
15. 8^3 = ____________
18. 11^2 = ____________

Main Idea and More

What to Know You can picture the main idea as a flag flying at the top of a pole. The flag is what you notice first. It's what's most important, just like the main idea. The flagpole holds up the flag, just as the details hold up, or support, the main idea. Details provide more facts about the main idea by offering reasons and giving examples.

Directions: Read the passage, then circle the correct main idea. Write the supporting details from the passage on the lines.

Instrucciones: Lee el pasaje, luego haz un círculo alrededor de la idea principal correcta. Escribe los detalles de apoyo del pasaje sobre las líneas.

The explorers held their flashlights high as they cautiously moved forward. No sooner had they stepped inside the tunnel than a great monster leaped from the shadows and blocked their way. The ugly beast had purple eyes. Above them, a horn rose from the center of its forehead. Its bright orange skin showed beneath a thin layer of coarse, black hair. As it reached its claws toward the terrified group, it snarled menacingly, revealing a mouthful of sharp teeth.

The main idea is:

a. The explorers discover a secret tunnel.

b. A frightening monster stands before the explorers.

c. An evil monster threatens to eat the explorers.

d. The frightened explorers need to use flashlights inside a dark tunnel.

The main idea is supported by these six details:

1. ______________________________

2. ______________________________

3. ______________________________

4. ______________________________

5. ______________________________

6. ______________________________

Solve the Riddle

Directions: Simplify each expression. Use the letters next to the problems to solve the riddle at the bottom of the page. Many letters will be used more than once while other letters will not be used at all.

Instrucciones: Simplifica cada expresión. Usa las letras al lado de los problemas para resolver el acertijo al final de la página. Muchas letras se usarán más de una vez, mientras que otras letras no serán usadas en absoluto.

H. $7 + (-5) =$ ________

Q. $-8 + 4 =$ ________

D. $4 + (-6) =$ ________

B. $-15 + (-3) =$ ________

F. $-28 + 28 =$ ________

G. $-9 - 2 =$ ________

O. $6 + (-9) =$ ________

W. $-7 + (-8) =$ ________

K. $-2 + (-4) =$ ________

X. $-15 + (-6) =$ ________

S. $-19 - (-18) =$ ________

A. $7 - 16 =$ ________

V. $-2 - (-8) =$ ________

U. $8 - (-3) =$ ________

E. $-9 + (-7) =$ ________

Y. $-2 + 7 =$ ________

J. $-18 + (-3) =$ ________

Z. $(6 - 2) - (-4) =$ ________

C. $5 \times 3 - (8 - 6) =$ ________

N. $6 - [2 - (-3)] =$ ________

M. $6 + [2 - (-4)] =$ ________

I. $32 + (-7) + (-30) =$ ________

P. $-31 + 62 + (-9) =$ ________

T. $33 + (-5) + (-25) =$ ________

R. $-5 + (-6) + (-9) =$ ________

L. $-20 + (-19) - 2 =$ ________

How many letters are there in the alphabet?

___ ___ ___ ___ ___ ___ :
−16 −41 −16 6 −16 1

___ ___ ___ ___ ___   ___ ___
3 2 −20 −16 −16   −5 1

“___ ___ ___”   ___ ___ ___
3 2 −16   −9 1 −2

___ ___ ___ ___ ___   ___ ___
−16 −5 −11 2 3   −5 1

“___ ___ ___ ___ ___ ___ ___ ___”
−9 −41 22 2 −9 −18 −16 3

Sentence Variety

Directions: In order to achieve sentence variety, change the order of the words in the following sentences without changing the meanings. Insert commas where they are needed.

Instrucciones: Para lograr variedad en las oraciones, cambia el orden de las palabras en las siguientes oraciones sin cambiar los significados. Inserta comas donde sean necesarias.

Example: I strolled to the neighborhood supermarket this morning to buy some milk.
This morning, I strolled to the neighborhood supermarket to buy some milk.

1. Do not go into the classroom unless you have permission first.

____

____

2. Henri could not go to the baseball game because he had the measles.

____

____

3. After the campers finished eating the hot dogs and marshmallows they roasted over the fire, they sat around telling ghost stories.

____

____

4. Louise picked up about twelve pounds of rocks when she went walking on Mora Beach.

____

____

5. Some of the banana slugs in the Hoh Rain Forest on the Olympic Peninsula are a foot long.

____

____

6. Before Tina could go to the movies, she had to wash the dishes, finish her homework, and clean her room.

____

____

7. Nearly every day, Fiona walks to school with her brother Ewan.

____

____

8. Every Tuesday from two until four in the afternoon, I practice playing the piano.

____

____

Positive and Negative

Directions: Compute the positive and negative values indicated in the problems below. Use the number line to help you with the easier amounts. Remember, always start at 0. Go to the right for positive values. Go to the left for negative values.

Instrucciones: Calcula los valores positivos y negativos indicados en los siguientes problemas. Utiliza la recta numérica para ayudarte con las cantidades más fáciles. Recuerda, siempre comienza en 0. Ve a la derecha para los valores positivos. Ve a la izquierda para los valores negativos.

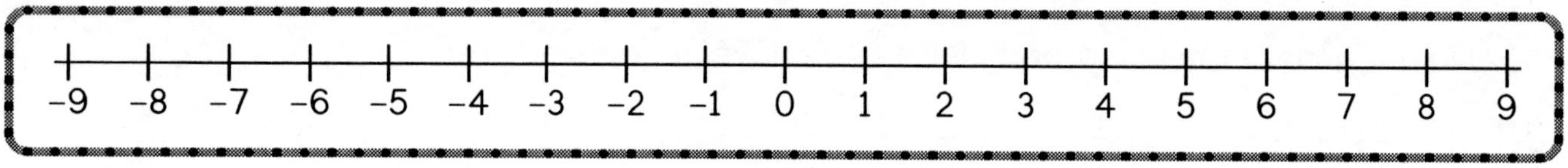

1. You have no money. You owe \$4 to your best friend. You earn \$5 doing chores.

   How much money will you have after you pay your friend? ____________________

2. John has no money, and he owes \$9 to his brother. He receives \$10 for his birthday.

   How much money does he have after paying back his brother? ____________________

3. Elizabeth has no money. She owes \$7 to Michelle and \$4 to Christine.

   How much money does she owe altogether? ____________________

4. What is the sum of –9 and 16? ____________________

5. James has no money, and he owes \$9 to Ronny and \$12 to Melissa.

   How much money does he owe altogether? ____________________

6. What is the sum of –10 and 12? ____________________

7. Irene has \$15 but she owes \$21 to her friend.

   How much will she still owe if she gives all her money to her friend? ____________________

8. What is the sum of –7 and –17? ____________________

9. George scored 9 points in one game and 8 points in a second game.

   What was his point total?____________________

10. What is the sum of –30 and –42? ____________________

11. What is the sum of –19 and –13? ____________________

12. Allison owes \$87 to the bank and \$139 to the credit card company.

    How much money does she owe altogether? ____________________

TV Guide

Directions: A TV guide is a list of programs arranged according to when they are aired. Use the *Pacific Post TV Guide* to answer the questions.

Instrucciones: Una guía de televisión es una lista de programas ordenados según el momento en que se emiten. Utiliza la *Pacific Post TV Guide* para responder las preguntas.

Saturday, January 22 — **Pacific Post TV Guide**

ABN Channel		NTV Channel		SBV Channel	
Noon	Sports World (includes reports from today's tennis, golf, bowling, and horse racing)	Noon	Midday Movie: Class of '10 (G)	Noon	Stage Divers (PG)
				1:00	Report from Britain (RPT)
		2:00	State Athletics: Championships		
				2:30	Sky Devils (G)
3:00	News Update			3:00	Top Golf Courses
3:15	Sports World				
		4:00	Lost in Space (RPT)	4:00	Theater News (G)
5:00	News and Weather			5:00	Pet Hotline (G)
5:30	What's Cooking? (G)	5:30	News and Weather	5:30	Cartoon Break (Y)
		6:00	Sports Review	6:00	News and Weather
6:30	Wildlife Park (G)	6:30	Holiday Line (G)	6:30	Just Stop It! (G)
7:30	Police Squad (RPT)	7:30	Our Street (Y)	7:30	Explorer Lost (G)
8:30	Art Report (MA)	8:30	Night Train (PG)	8:30	Movie: Ozone (PG)

Programs			
	Y – All Children	PG – Parental Guidance	RPT – Repeat
	G – General Audience	MA – Mature Audience	S – Subtitles

1. Which channel has news at 3 p.m.? ______
2. How long is *Our Street* on NTV? __________
3. Is *Art Report* suitable for children? _______
4. Which channel has the most sports? _____
5. What does "RPT" stand for? ______________________
6. How many parental guidance shows are scheduled to air? ______________
7. Name a program that requires parental guidance. ______________________
8. If I watched *Police Squad,* I would miss *Night Train.* ☐ True ☐ False
9. The first news program is on at 5:30 p.m. ☐ True ☐ False
10. The *Sports World* program is interrupted by a *News Update.* ☐ True ☐ False
11. What day is this program for? ____
12. Which show follows the *NTV Sports Review*? ____

Follow the Formulas

Directions: Compute the positive and negative values indicated in the problems below.

Instrucciones: Calcula los valores positivos y negativos indicados en los problemas.

Formulas to Know

- negative × negative = positive (Example: $-3 \times -6 = 18$)
- positive × negative = negative (Example: $4 \times -5 = -20$)
- negative ÷ negative = positive (Example: $-36 \div -4 = 9$)
- positive ÷ negative = negative (Example: $24 \div -3 = -8$)
- negative ÷ positive = negative (Example: $-42 \div 7 = -6$)

1. Jill owes $4 to Jennifer, $4 to Michelle, and $4 to Eileen.

   How much does she owe altogether? ______________________

2. Joey owes $5 to 4 different friends.

   How much money does he owe altogether? ______________________

3. What is the product of –7 and –6? ______________________

4. The total bill at a restaurant was $49, to be split evenly among 7 friends.

   How much money did each friend owe? ______________________

5. How much is –81 divided by 9? ______________________

6. How much is –100 divided by –10? ______________________

7. Each of 18 patrons owes $15 at a restaurant.

   What is the total amount owed by all 18 customers? ______________________

8. What is the product of –12 and –13? ______________________

9. How much is –16 times 4? ______________________

10. What is the quotient when –45 is divided by –9? ______________________

11. A group of 15 teenagers owes $75 at a pizza parlor.

    If they split the bill evenly, how much will each person owe? ______________________

12. How much is –200 divided by –10? ______________________

Cause and Effect

Directions: Complete the chart below. The left side of the chart is for causes, and the right side of the chart is for effects. Make sure that your answers make sense.

Instrucciones: Completa el cuadro de abajo. El lado izquierdo del gráfico es para causas, y el lado derecho de la tabla es para efectos. Asegúrate que tus respuestas tengan sentido.

Causes	Effects
1. I tripped on the steps at school.	1. ______________________
2. ______________________	2. We were soaking wet!
3. I scored the winning goal in our soccer game.	3. ______________________
4. ______________________	4. My mom is very happy today.
5. I completed my homework.	5. ______________________

If True, Then Do

Directions: To solve the puzzle and find the hidden abbreviation, read the sentences below. If the statement is true, color the numbered puzzle spaces as directed.

Instrucciones: Para resolver el rompecabezas y encontrar la abreviatura escondida, lee las oraciones. Si la declaración es verdadera, colorea los espacios numerados del rompecabezas como se indica.

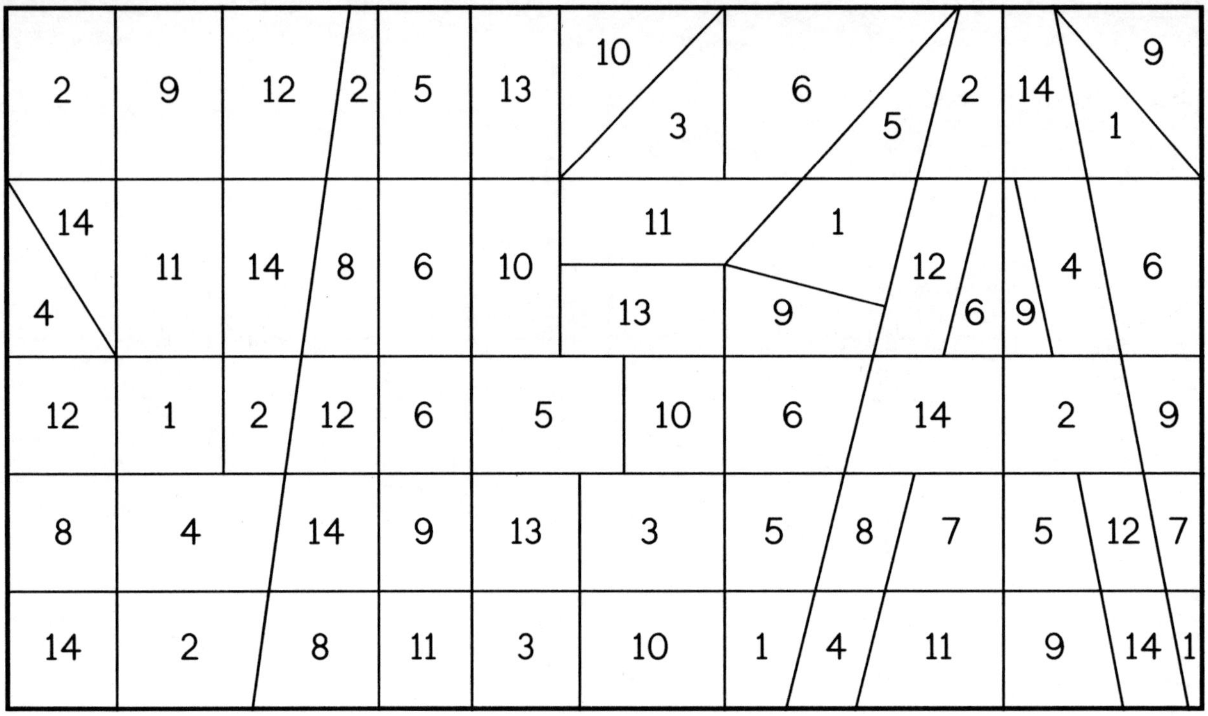

- If Mississippi is an ocean, color the #1 spaces blue.
- If Tennessee is a state, color the #2 spaces red.
- If Hawaii is a state, color the #3 spaces blue.
- If Mexico is a country, color the #4 spaces red.
- If Michigan is a country, color the #5 spaces red.
- If Florida is a river, color the #6 spaces blue.
- If Kentucky is in South America, color the #7 spaces red.
- If Canada is a country, color the #8 spaces red.
- If England is a continent, color the #9 spaces blue.
- If Washington is a state, color the #10 spaces blue.
- If Ohio is an island, color the #11 spaces blue.
- If New York is a city, color the #12 spaces red.
- If California borders an ocean, color the #13 spaces blue.
- If Australia is an island, color the #14 spaces red.

What abbreviation did you find?

____

Sports Stumpers

Directions: Find the name of the football, basketball, baseball, or hockey team that fits each clue. Choose your answer from the Team List.

Instrucciones: Encuentra el nombre del equipo de fútbol, baloncesto, béisbol o hockey que se ajuste a cada clave. Elige tu respuesta de la "Team List".

Team List				
	A's	Dodgers	Patriots	Suns
	Avalanche	49ers	Rockets	Timberwolves
	Bucks	Heat	Sharks	Twins
	Bulls			

1. This team is proud to be American. ____________________
2. This team looks like another team. ____________________
3. This team travels in packs. ____________________
4. This team can bury you alive. ____________________
5. This team can blast into space. ____________________
6. This team gets out of the way. ____________________
7. This team loves the water. ____________________
8. This team could be deer or dollar bills. ____________________
9. Each year, this team runs through the streets of Spain. ____________________
10. This team gets good grades. ____________________
11. This team is always looking for gold. ____________________
12. These two teams will not leave you cold. ____________________

____

Order of Operations

Directions: Evaluate the expressions. Be sure to follow the order of operations listed below. Circle your final answers. The first one has been done for you.

Instrucciones: Evalúa las expresiones. Asegúrate de seguir el orden de las operaciones que se enumeran a continuación. Haz un círculo alrededor de tus respuestas finales. El ejemplo es para ti.

Order of Operations

Evaluate expressions in this order: **PEMDAS**

- **P**arentheses: Do these operations first.
- **E**xponents: Find these values next.
- **M**ultiply and **D**ivide: Go in order from left to right.
- **A**dd and **S**ubtract: Go in order from left to right.

1. $4^2 + 9 - (3 \times 5)$ $4^2 + 9 - 15$ $16 + 9 - 15$ $25 - 15 = 10$	**2.** $6^2 - (9 \times 2) + 12$	**3.** $10 + (8 \times 3) - 3^2$
4. $(8 \times 8) - 4^3 + 1$	**5.** $8^2 + (4 \times 5) - 21$	**6.** $(9 \times 5) - 2^3 + 16$
7. $15 \div (7 - 2^2) + 1$	**8.** $(9 + 11) - 3^2 + 7$	**9.** $(6 \times 5) - 2^3 + 16$
10. $12^2 - (9 \times 12) - 4^2$	**11.** $13^2 - (11 \times 9) + 16$	**12.** $13 + (6 \times 8) - 5^2$
13. $17 - (9 + 8) + 2^3$	**14.** $9^2 - (27 + 13) - 6^2$	**15.** $44 - (7 \times 6) + 4^2$

Word Choice

Directions: Replace the underlined words with more appropriate or more specific words. The first one has been done for you.

Instrucciones: Reemplaza las palabras subrayadas con palabras más apropiadas o específicas. El ejemplo es para ti.

1. Sanford said that he would be there later.

   Sanford growled that he would be at Commonwealth Park later.

2. Josefina liked the dress.

   ____

3. Betty walked to the store.

   ____

4. The music was terrific.

   ____

5. Lim asked the man for food.

   ____

6. Beverly ate three sandwiches.

   ____

7. Several children skipped happily away.

   ____

8. Suzi thanked her nicely.

   ____

9. The horse ran around the corral.

   ____

10. Nolan talked with the pretty fashion model.

    ____

11. Not wanting to be late for the important occasion, he ran.

    ____

Polygon Perimeters

Directions: Compute the perimeter of the shapes below.

Instrucciones: Calcula el perímetro de las siguientes formas.

What to Know

The perimeter of a parallelogram is computed by adding the length plus the width and multiplying the sum by two.

perimeter of a parallelogram = 2 × (length + width)

1.

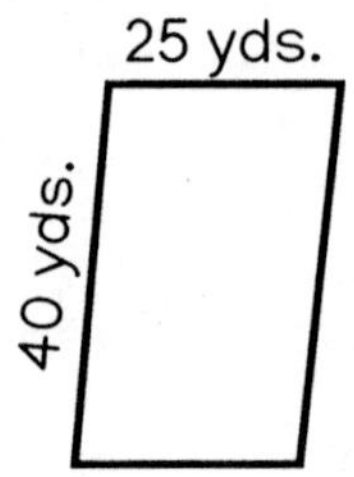

____

2.

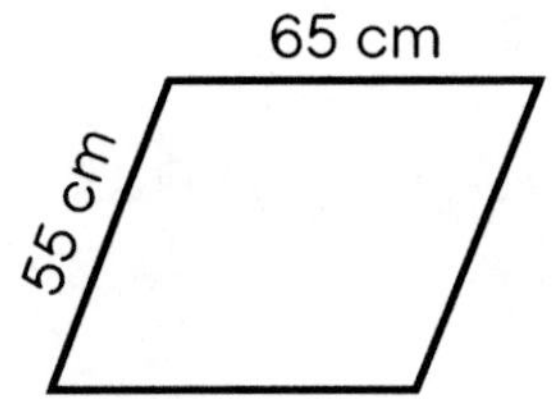

____

3.

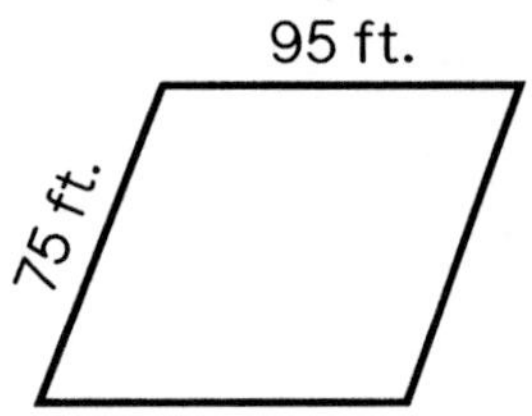

____

4.

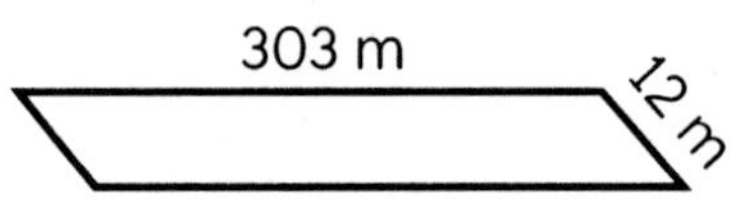

____

5.

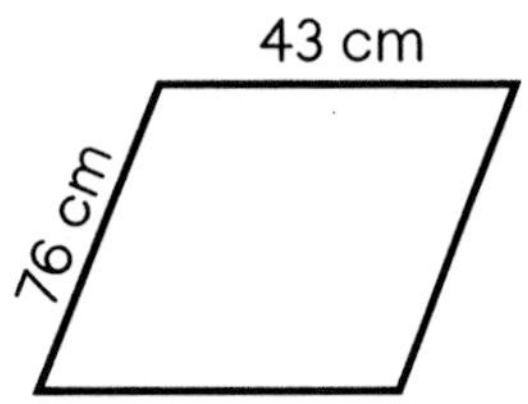

____

6.

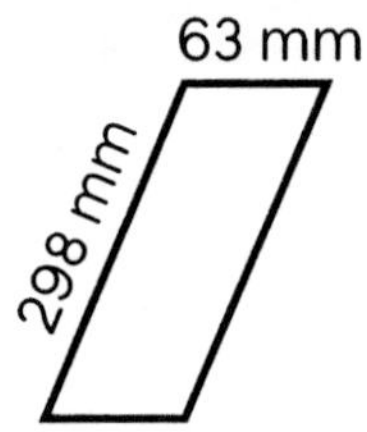

____

7.

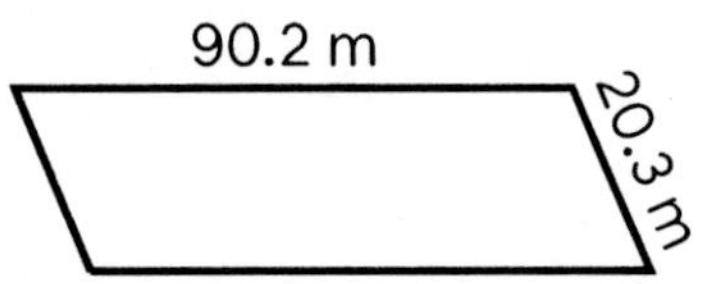

____

8.

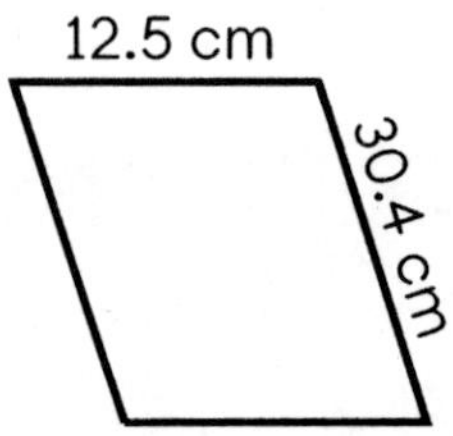

____

The Birds

Directions: Read the passage, then circle the correct answers below.

Instrucciones: Lee el párrafo, luego haz un círculo alrededor de las respuestas correctas.

There once was a farmer who planted fresh fields of wheat. He cared for the wheat and ensured that it received adequate amounts of water, sun, and nourishment. His livelihood depended on this crop of wheat.

One morning, the farmer awoke to the sound of birds in his field. From his window, he saw his wheat field covered with birds. In a panic, he ran outside and began flapping his arms and making loud sounds. He hoped that this would scare the birds away. His plan worked. The birds flew away in a flurry, and the farmer went back about his work.

Early the next morning, the farmer was again awakened to the sound of birds. He followed the same procedure and scared the birds by making loud noises and flapping his arms. It worked again. The birds flew away and left his wheat alone.

The birds began to realize that they were never in any real danger. They realized the farmer walked around waving at them and making sounds. The birds got braver and braver.

On the third morning, the farmer heard the birds again and realized that he needed to be more severe. He grabbed his dog's collar and headed outside. The birds did not even move. They knew he would try to scare them, so they weren't too worried. The farmer let his dog loose, and the dog chased the birds. This frightened the birds, and they flew away, never to be seen again.

1. What is the moral of the story?
   - a. What goes around comes around.
   - b. Work before play.
   - c. If at first you don't succeed, try, try again.
   - d. The early bird gets the worm.

2. What would be a good title for this reading passage?
   - a. "The Last Resort"
   - b. "The Two Sides"
   - c. "Planting Seeds"
   - d. "Anger Always Works First"

3. Locate the statement below that did *not* happen in the story.
   - a. The farmer was trying to attract the birds.
   - b. The farmer was awakened by the sound of birds.
   - c. The farmer knew that he had to show the birds he meant business.
   - d. The birds were not afraid of the farmer.

Mow Area

Directions: Lawn Magic is a business run by three sixth-grade friends who earn money mowing their neighbors' lawns. They charge by the square foot, so they need to know the area of each lawn they mow. Help Lawn Magic compute the area in square feet of each lawn described below.

Instrucciones: "Lawn Magic" es un negocio dirigido por tres amigos de sexto grado que ganan dinero podandolos jardines de sus vecinos. Cobran por pie cuadrado, por lo que necesitan saber el área de cada césped que cortan. Ayuda a "Lawn Magic" a calcular el área en pies cuadrados de cada césped descrito a continuación.

Formulas to Know

- **area of a rectangle** = base × height (or length × width)
- **area of a parallelogram** = base × height
- **area of a triangle** = base × height ÷ 2

1. Lawn Magic did your neighbor's lawn, which is a rectangular shape 12 feet high and 20 feet long at the base. What is the area? ______________ square feet
2. Lawn Magic mowed Mr. Crick's parallelogram-shaped lawn, which has a height of 15 feet and a base of 30 feet. What is the area? ______________ square feet
3. Mr. Ford's lawn is a parallelogram with a height of 23 feet and a base of 45 feet. What is the area Lawn Magic will mow? ______________ square feet
4. Mrs. Jopp's lawn is triangular with a height of 12 feet and a base of 40 feet. What is the area that Lawn Magic will mow? ______________ square feet
5. Lawn Magic mowed Mr. Lee's front lawn, which is a rectangle 43 feet high and 97 feet long at the base. What is the area they mowed? ______________ square feet
6. Mr. Dapper's back lawn is a triangle with a height of 33 feet and a base of 70 feet. What is the area? ______________ square feet
7. Mrs. Smith's side lawn is a parallelogram 22.4 feet high and 30 feet long at the base. What is the area Lawn Magic will mow? ______________ square feet
8. Lawn Magic mowed Ms. Brown's front lawn, a triangle 12.5 feet high and 14 feet long at the base. What is the area they mowed? ______________ square feet
9. What is the area of a triangular lawn 16.6 feet high and 12 feet at the base? ______________ square feet
10. What is the area of a square lawn 22 feet on each side? ______________ square feet

Irregular Verbs

Many verbs end in *–ed* when you put them into the past tense. However, for some verbs, you do not simply add an *–ed* to put them into past tense. These are called *irregular verbs*. Here are some examples:

Present Tense	spy	hide	bring
Past Tense	spied	hid	brought

Directions: Write the following irregular verbs in the past tense.

Instrucciones: Escribe los siguientes verbos irregulares en tiempo pasado.

1. fly ______________
2. swim ______________
3. cry ______________
4. drink ______________
5. go ______________
6. speed ______________
7. run ______________
8. sing ______________
9. draw ______________
10. eat ______________
11. buy ______________
12. speak ______________
13. ride ______________
14. wear ______________
15. grow ______________
16. freeze ______________
17. make ______________
18. sleep ______________

Other words in the sentence can give clues as to which tense the verb should be. Words such as *yesterday*, *last month*, and *previously* show that the action occurred in the past. Words such as *tomorrow*, *in the future*, and *next week* show that the action will occur in the future.

Directions: Add a verb to each of the sentences below. Make sure your choice is in the appropriate tense.

Instrucciones: Agrega un verbo a cada una de las siguientes oraciones. Asegúrate que tu elección esté en el tiempo apropiado.

19. Last week, we ______________ to the opera.
20. Today, I ______________ exhausted and I can't stop yawning.
21. In 2010, my family ______________ a huge party.
22. Riley ______________ whenever he's told to do chores.
23. Fluffy always ______________ under his bed when it's time for his bath.
24. Tomorrow, we ______________ to the movies.
25. In the year 3000, people ______________ on Mars.
26. Yesterday, I ______________ twenty dollars.

Finding the Volume

Directions: Find the volume for each rectangular solid.

Instrucciones: Encuentra el volumen de cada rectángulo sólido.

Formula to Know volume of a rectangular solid = length × width × height

V = l × w × h

1.

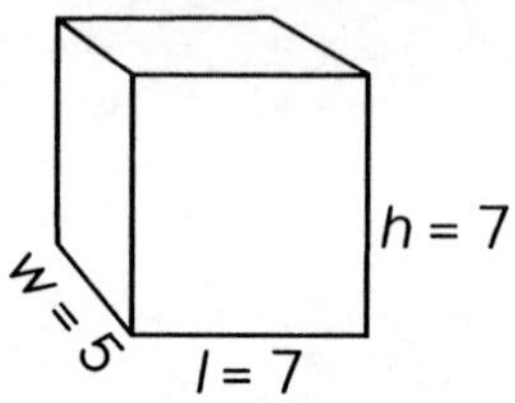

______ × ______ × ______ =

__________ cubic units

2.

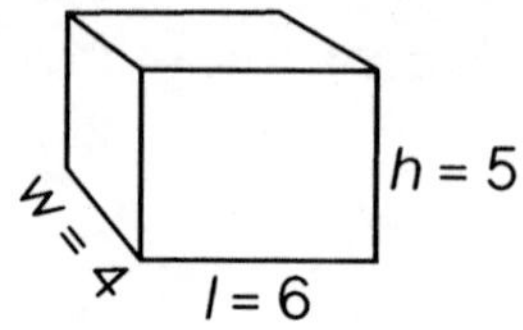

______ × ______ × ______ =

__________ cubic units

3.

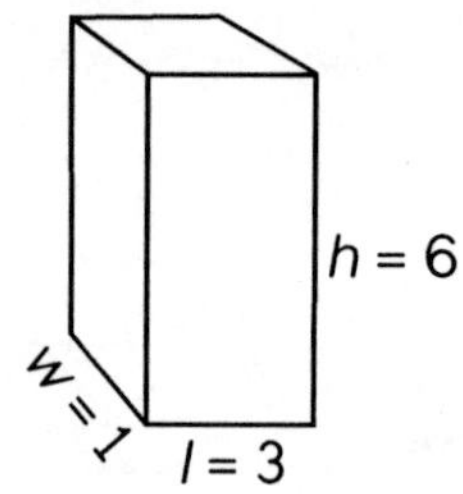

______ × ______ × ______ =

__________ cubic units

Directions: Find the volume for each cube.

Instrucciones: Encuentra el volumen de cada cubo.

Formula to Know Volume of a cube = side × side × side

$V = s^3$

4.

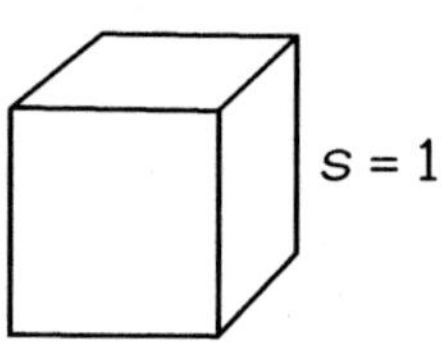

$\_\_\_^3 =$

__________ cubic unit

5.

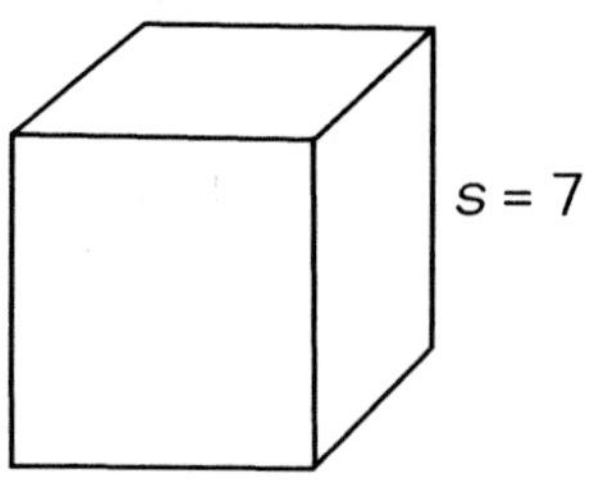

$\_\_\_^3 =$

__________ cubic unit

6.

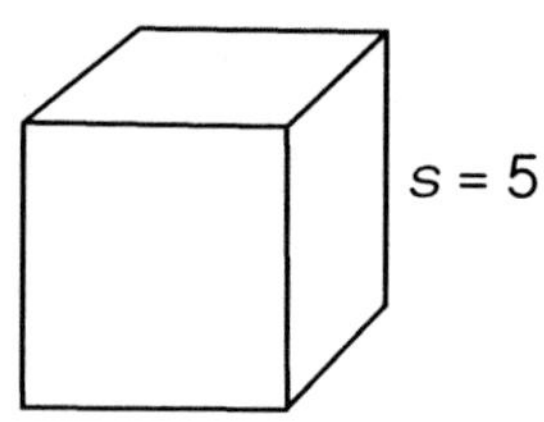

$\_\_\_^3 =$

__________ cubic unit

Verb Vocabulary

Mini Dictionary

accumulate – to gather or acquire more and more of something

anticipate – to expect something to happen

calculate – to use math to determine

contribute – to add to or to help something come about

exaggerate – represent something as being larger, better, or worse than it is

irrigate – to supply with water or other liquid

retrieve – to get or bring back

substitute – to add something or someone in the place of another

Directions: Use the Mini Dictionary to help you determine each answer.

Instrucciones: Usa el "Mini Dictionary" para ayudarte a determinar cada respuesta.

1. Farmers must do this to their crops to help them grow. ____________
2. Someone might do this to make a story more incredible. ____________
3. A person who collects baseball cards would do this. ____________
4. Someone finding the area of a polygon does this. ____________
5. Teammates giving $1 each to buy a ball do this. ____________
6. Someone replacing old batteries with new ones does this. ____________
7. A child hoping to get a toy for their birthday does this. ____________
8. A dog bringing a thrown stick back to its owner does this. ____________

Directions: Fill in each sentence with the best word from the Mini Dictionary.

Instrucciones: Completa cada oración con la mejor palabra del "Mini Dictionary".

9. If everyone can ____________ one hour of their time, we can clean up the park.
10. I left my wallet at home, so I must go back to ____________ it.
11. I think you ____________ when you call that movie the worst thing ever.
12. Can you help me ____________ the distance between here and the airport?
13. My goal is to ____________ as many points as it takes to earn the top prize.
14. I always ____________ avocado for chicken when I order that salad.
15. I do not ____________ this game ending for at least another hour.
16. Dr. Wu had to ____________ Tom's eye to flush out the irritation.

Homophone Search

Directions: For each of the words listed, write its homophone. Then, find those homophones in the puzzle below. The first one is done for you.

Instrucciones: Para cada una de las palabras enumeradas, escribe su homófono. Luego, encuentra esos homófonos en el rompecabezas de abajo. El ejemplo es para ti.

1. aloud allowed
2. ate ____
3. ball ____
4. chews ____
5. coarse ____
6. days ____
7. deer ____
8. hare ____
9. hole ____
10. jean ____
11. leased ____
12. made ____
13. main ____
14. night ____
15. paws ____
16. red ____
17. scene ____
18. stake ____
19. steal ____
20. strait ____

A	D	I	W	M	V	E	S	R	U	O	C	S
H	L	W	H	O	L	E	M	T	O	B	U	J
G	D	L	Y	T	G	T	X	N	M	A	I	D
H	E	W	O	L	D	A	E	R	A	Z	N	X
Y	A	B	A	W	L	K	E	I	U	E	R	K
T	R	L	H	S	E	M	E	G	E	S	A	N
K	S	G	E	N	E	D	C	S	H	C	E	I
M	O	H	D	A	T	P	A	T	O	T	I	G
A	P	A	M	N	S	R	Z	E	T	O	G	H
N	Z	I	W	O	S	T	R	A	I	G	H	T
E	G	R	P	A	U	S	E	K	Z	L	T	C

Homophone Crossword

Directions: Write the homophones for the given words in the puzzle below. One word has been done for you.

Instrucciones: Escribe los homófonos de las palabras dadas en el siguiente rompecabezas. Una de las palabras se da como ejemplo para ti.

Across

2. ate
5. chili
6. piece
7. plumb
11. forth
13. vein/vane
15. write/rite
16. maid
17. paws

Down

~~1. bin~~
3. tow
4. wood
5. sense/scents
6. pour/pore
7. principle
8. knight
9. borne
8. knight
9. borne
10. their/they're
12. patients
14. sail

Geometry Quiz

Directions: Read each problem carefully. Circle the correct answer.

Instrucciones: Lee cada problema cuidadosamente. Haz un círculo alrededor de la respuesta correcta.

1. What are these lines called?
   - a. intersecting
   - b. parallel
   - c. perpendicular
   - d. crossing

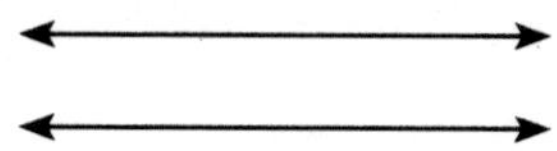

2. What are these lines called?
   - a. parallel
   - b. perpendicular
   - c. crossing
   - d. segments

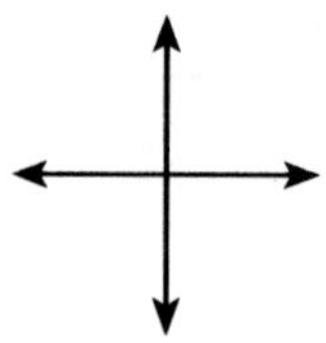

3. What kind of angle is this?
   - a. obtuse
   - b. acute
   - c. 30 degree
   - d. right

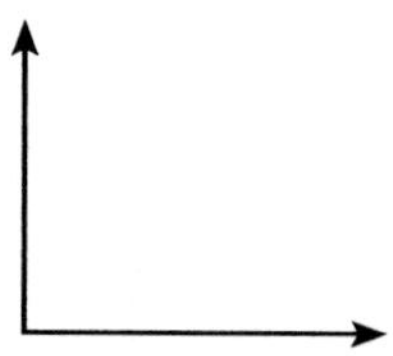

4. Which angle is less than 90 degrees?
   - a. obtuse
   - b. right
   - c. acute
   - d. sharp

5. What is the name of this angle?
   - a. ∠DEF
   - b. ∠EFD
   - c. ∠FED
   - d. both a and c

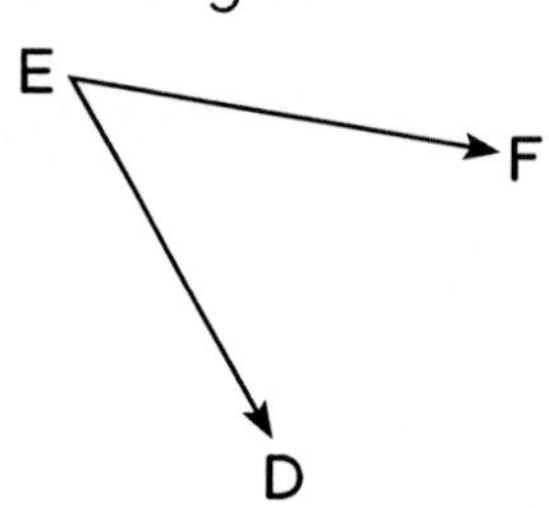

6. Two angles that add up to 180 degrees are called what?
   - a. supplementary
   - b. complementary
   - c. both of these
   - d. none of these

7. What kind of a triangle is this?
   - a. isosceles
   - b. scalene
   - c. equilateral
   - d. none of these

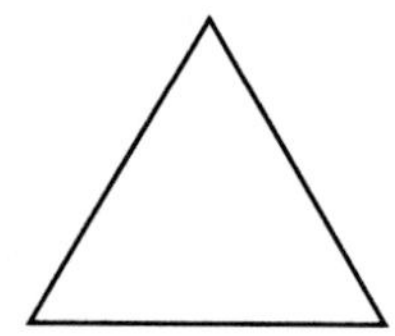

8. What defines a scalene triangle?
   - a. It has two sides of equal length.
   - b. It has three sides of equal length.
   - c. It is pointy.
   - d. It has no sides of equal length.

9. What is this called?
   - a. ray line
   - b. line
   - c. line segment
   - d. end point

10. What kinds of lines are these?
    - a. adjacent
    - b. intersecting
    - c. infinity
    - d. perpendicular

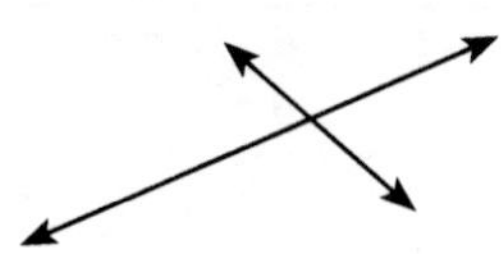

The Longest River

Directions: Read the passage below, then circle the correct answers.

Instrucciones: Lee el párrafo, luego haz un círculo alrededor de las respuestas correctas.

Ancient Egyptian life centered around the life-giving waters of the Nile, the longest river in the world. Every Egyptian, from the poorest peasant to the pharaoh, depended on the Nile, as its banks contained the only land with soil able to grow crops.

The Egyptians took full advantage of the Nile River. People were able to live secure in the knowledge that they were safe from intruders who didn't dare cross the deserts that surrounded their fertile valleys. Because of the annual flooding, the Egyptians were able to establish a fairly regular cycle of planting and harvesting. Excess crops were then exported, making Egypt a wealthy nation. Animals thrived in the waters and surrounding land of the Nile. Goods were easily transported on barges and ferries. Probably the most valuable gift of the Nile was papyrus, a tall reed which grew along its banks. Papyrus was used to make paper, and Egypt was the sole supplier of this product until rag paper was invented in the 12th century.

1. Who depended on the Nile?
   a. the pharaoh
   b. the farmers
   c. the peasants
   d. all of the above

2. According to the passage, what did the Nile do that helped the Egyptians establish a farming cycle?
   a. It ran into channels they had created to water their crops.
   b. It flooded each year.
   c. It dried out each year, so the farmers could use the riverbed for farming.
   d. It kept the farm animals alive.

3. According to the passage, how did the Nile help make the Egyptians wealthy?
   a. The Egyptians could produce enough crops to sell to other countries.
   b. The Egyptians could produce enough crops to feed their families.
   c. The Egyptians could pan for gold in the Nile.
   d. The Egyptians bottled the water from the Nile and sold it.

4. According to the passage, the most valuable gift of the Nile was probably
   a. water.
   b. the animals who lived on the Nile.
   c. papyrus.
   d. the crops that the Nile produced.

Coordinates Code

How do you make a hot dog stand?

Directions: The answer to this riddle is written in a special code at the bottom of this page. Each pair of numbers stands for a point on the graph. The first number in an ordered pair tells you how far to go across the coordinate plane, and the second number tells you how far up to go. Write the letter shown near the point at the intersection of each pair of numbers. The letters will spell out the answer to the riddle.

Instrucciones: La respuesta a este acertijo está escrita en un código especial al final de esta página. Cada par de números representa un punto en el gráfico. El primer número en un par ordenado te dice qué tan lejos cruzar el plano de coordenadas, y el segundo número te dice qué tan lejos arriba para ir. Escribe la letra que se muestra cerca del punto en la intersección de cada par de números. Las letras te mostrarán la respuesta al acertijo.

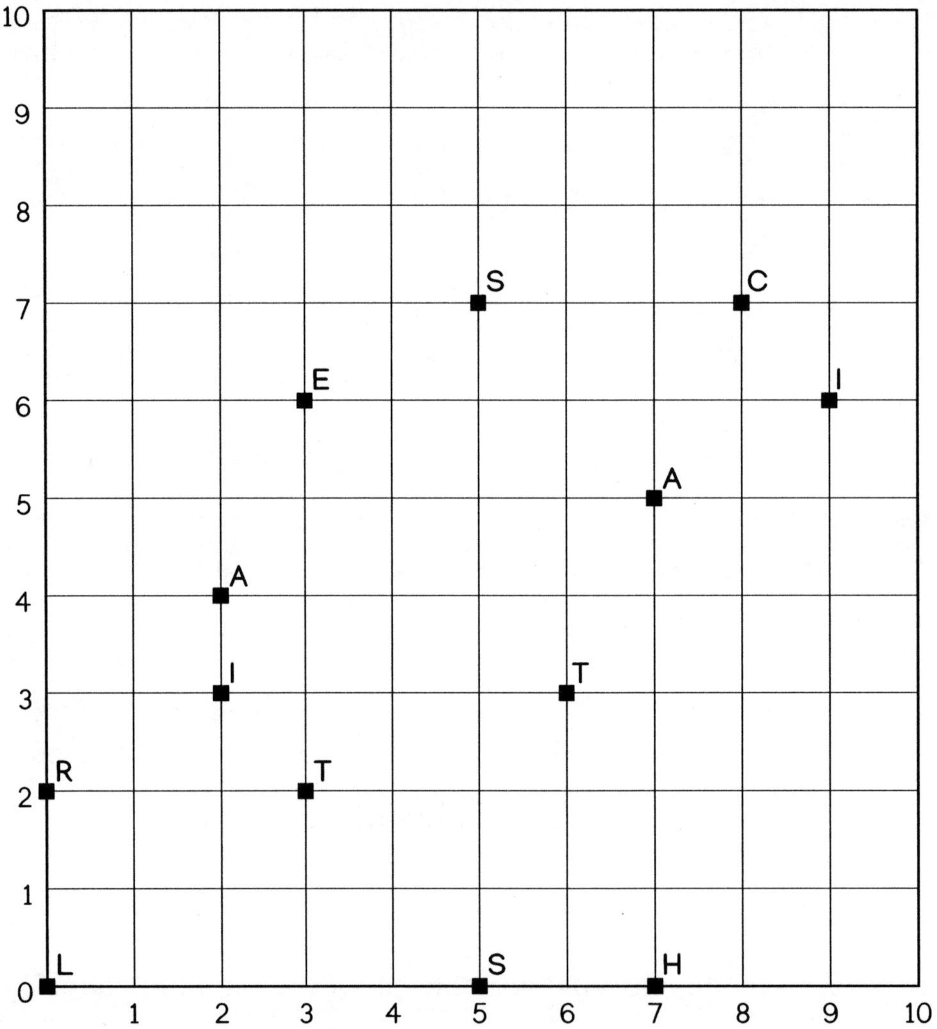

___ ___ ___ ___ ___　___ ___ ___　___ ___ ___ ___ ___
(5, 7) (6, 3) (3, 6) (7, 5) (0, 0)　(2, 3) (3, 2) (5, 0)　(8, 7) (7, 0) (2, 4) (9, 6) (0, 2)

Sentence Fragments

What to Know

Sentence fragments occur when a sentence is missing either a subject or a verb. Sentence fragments are also called *incomplete sentences.*

Examples: *Incorrect*—Going to the circus tomorrow.

Problem—Who is going to the circus? The sentence is missing a subject.

Correction—Judy and Flanders are going to the circus tomorrow.

Incorrect—My two cats, Iago and Alger.

Problem—What action is occurring? The sentence is missing a verb.

Correction—My two cats, Iago and Alger, love to sleep.

Directions: Study the sentence fragments below. Decide whether each sentence fragment is missing a subject or a verb. Write "subject" or "verb" in the space beside each sentence fragment.

Instrucciones: Estudia los fragmentos de oración a continuación. Decide si en cada fragmento de oración falta un sujeto o un verbo. Escribe "subject" o "verb" en el espacio al lado de cada fragmento de oración.

1. Are watching the hockey game. ______________________
2. Is an excellent actress. ______________________
3. Can juggle six apples. ______________________
4. The old, battered suitcase. ______________________
5. Los Angeles, California. ______________________
6. The red convertible. ______________________

Directions: Rewrite each fragment. Add either a subject or a verb to make a complete sentence.

Instrucciones: Vuelve a escribir el fragmento. Agrega un sujeto o un verbo par completar la oración.

1. ____
2. ____
3. ____
4. ____
5. ____
6. ____

Writing Coordinates

Directions: Write the coordinate for each point on the grid below.

Instrucciones: Escribe la coordenada para cada punto en la cuadricula.

1. K = ________	**4.** L = ________	**7.** H = ________	**10.** C = ________
2. D = ________	**5.** E = ________	**8.** B = ________	**11.** A = ________
3. G = ________	**6.** I = ________	**9.** F = ________	**12.** J = ________

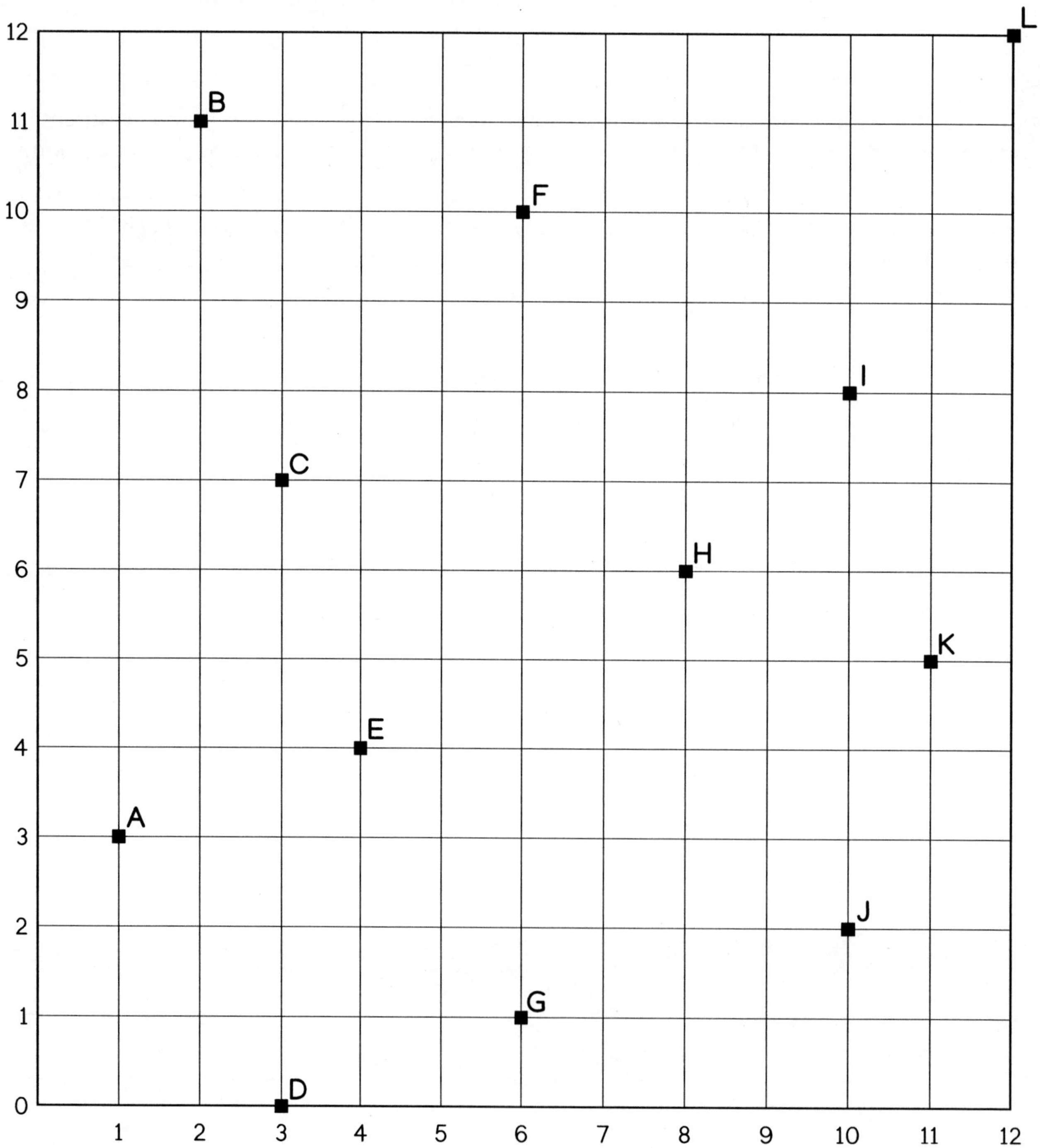

The Green Revolution

Directions: This passage is an excerpt from the book *Earth First* by David Bowden and Jenny Dibley. Read the passage, then answer the questions below.

Instrucciones: Este pasaje es un extracto del libro *Earth First* de David Bowden y Jenny Dibley. Lee el pasaje, luego responde las preguntas.

There is a revolution taking place in the minds of consumers around the world. It is known as the "green revolution" or the era of environmentally–friendly shopping.

In the past, many consumers have not given their shopping habits and choices much thought. The need to think about what happens to products when they have been used has not, until recently, been an issue of concern.

In the past few years, however, consumers have become much more conscious of the impact of their shopping habits. People are now discussing the environment in terms of how everyone has a role to play in reversing this damage. Every time we buy a product, we consume resources that in some way deplete the environment. This is why it is time to rethink our shopping habits and choices.

There are many points to consider when buying a product. The cost of a product is usually the most important consideration for consumers. Comfort, size, shape, how fashionable the product is, and how it compares with similar products in terms of quality, are also important.

The "green consumer" will also consider how the use of the product being purchased will affect the environment. Today's consumers should ask themselves the following questions before selecting a product:

- Has an animal suffered or died to make it?
- Were harmful chemicals used to make it?
- Can it be reused or recycled after it is used?
- Is it made from recycled materials?
- Is it overpackaged?
- Is it really necessary?

1. According to the excerpt, the "green revolution" is mainly concerned with
   a. the cost of goods in supermarkets.
   b. whether or not goods are made from recycled material.
   c. how the production of a product will affect the environment.
   d. the amount of unnecessary packaging on many items.

2. A "green consumer" is one who
   a. will not buy goods from a supermarket.
   b. considers many points before making a purchase.
   c. reuses all the packaging that comes with a purchase.
   d. will only damage the environment if the goods are not expensive.

3. For some shoppers, fashion is more important than the environment. ☐ True ☐ False

4. Which of the story's six bullet points do you consider to be most important? Why?

____

____

Dividing Fractions

Directions: Divide the fractions below. Write your answers in lowest terms.

Instrucciones: Divide las siguientes fracciones. Escribe tus respuestas en los términos menores.

1. $3\frac{2}{3} \div 4\frac{2}{3} =$	9. $\frac{3}{10} \div \frac{12}{30} =$	17. $2\frac{1}{3} \div \frac{3}{4} =$
2. $4\frac{3}{7} \div 2\frac{4}{7} =$	10. $\frac{1}{5} \div \frac{4}{15} =$	18. $3\frac{3}{4} \div \frac{3}{5} =$
3. $2\frac{1}{3} \div 3\frac{1}{6} =$	11. $\frac{13}{20} \div \frac{3}{10} =$	19. $6\frac{1}{2} \div \frac{2}{3} =$
4. $5\frac{6}{7} \div 6\frac{3}{14} =$	12. $\frac{2}{7} \div \frac{2}{3} =$	20. $1\frac{1}{2} \div 6 =$
5. $3\frac{3}{5} \div 5\frac{4}{5} =$	13. $\frac{4}{9} \div \frac{2}{5} =$	21. $\frac{5}{7} \div 3\frac{4}{5} =$
6. $\frac{5}{6} \div \frac{2}{3} =$	14. $\frac{4}{9} \div \frac{1}{2} =$	22. $\frac{1}{4} \div 3\frac{1}{5} =$
7. $\frac{1}{4} \div \frac{3}{8} =$	15. $\frac{8}{9} \div \frac{3}{4} =$	23. $2\frac{3}{8} \div \frac{4}{5} =$
8. $\frac{5}{12} \div \frac{2}{24} =$	16. $\frac{3}{6} \div 1\frac{2}{3} =$	24. $3\frac{3}{4} \div \frac{1}{9} =$

All About Adjectives

What to Know

Adjectives are words that describe either nouns or pronouns. They answer these questions: *What kind? How many? Which one? How much?*

Examples: She wore a *silver* ring on her finger. *(What kind?)*
We served dinner to *forty* people. *(How many?)*
Charles always chooses the *biggest* piece of cake. *(Which one?)*
I need to buy *three boxes* of sugar. *(How much?)*

Directions: Rewrite the following sentences, adding adjectives to answer the questions.

Instrucciones: Vuelve a escribir las siguientes oraciones, agregando adjetivos para responder las preguntas.

1. Georgina likes her dance class. *(What kind?)*

   ____

2. People crowded into the stadium for the concert. *(How many?)*

   ____

3. I won the stuffed bear. *(Which one?)*

   ____

4. Mickey did math homework. *(How much?)*

   ____

There are three types of adjectives:

- Common adjectives describe nouns or pronouns.
  Example: The *strong* woman lifted boxes into the truck.
- Proper adjectives are formed from proper nouns.
  Example: She studied *Egyptian* art in college.
- Compound adjectives are made up of more than one word. They are sometimes hyphenated.
  Examples: My brother lives in a *far-off* place.

Directions: Add adjectives to these sentences, according to the type listed.

Instrucciones: Agrega adjetivos a estas oraciones, según el tipo enumerado.

5. My ____________________ brother hates avocados and tomatoes. *(common)*

6. Tom found a ______________________________ clover. *(compound)*

7. Every summer, we go to the ________________________ Ocean. *(proper)*

8. Her ____________________________ dress cost twenty dollars. *(common)*

Neighbor Numbers

Directions: Find each person's apartment number and write it on the lines.

Instrucciones: Encuentra el número de departamento de cada persona y escríbelo en las líneas.

Clues

- Brandon lives directly across from Matt and in between Violet and Maria.
- Louisa lives in an even-numbered apartment.
- Gary lives directly across from Violet.
- Maria does not live directly across from Gary or Matt.
- Brandon lives in an odd-numbered apartment.
- Maria lives in apartment number 215.

________________	________________	________________
210	**212**	**214**
211	**213**	**215**
________________	________________	________________

Matt lives in apartment number ______________.

Brandon lives in apartment number ______________.

Gary lives in apartment number ______________.

Louisa lives in apartment number ______________.

Maria lives in apartment number ______________.

Violet lives in apartment number ______________.

More Map Madness!

Do you see Juanita? She is lost again! Follow the directions to get her back on track. Mark her ending spot with an **X**.

¿Ves a Juanita? ¡Se ha vuelto a perder! Sigue las instrucciones para que vuelva al camino. Marca punto final con una **X**.

Directions:

1. Take Hennepin Ave. south.
2. Turn east on E. 7th St.
3. Head north on 2nd Ave. S.
4. Go east on E. 3rd St.
5. Go south on 5th Ave. S.
6. END End at the corner of E. 8th St.

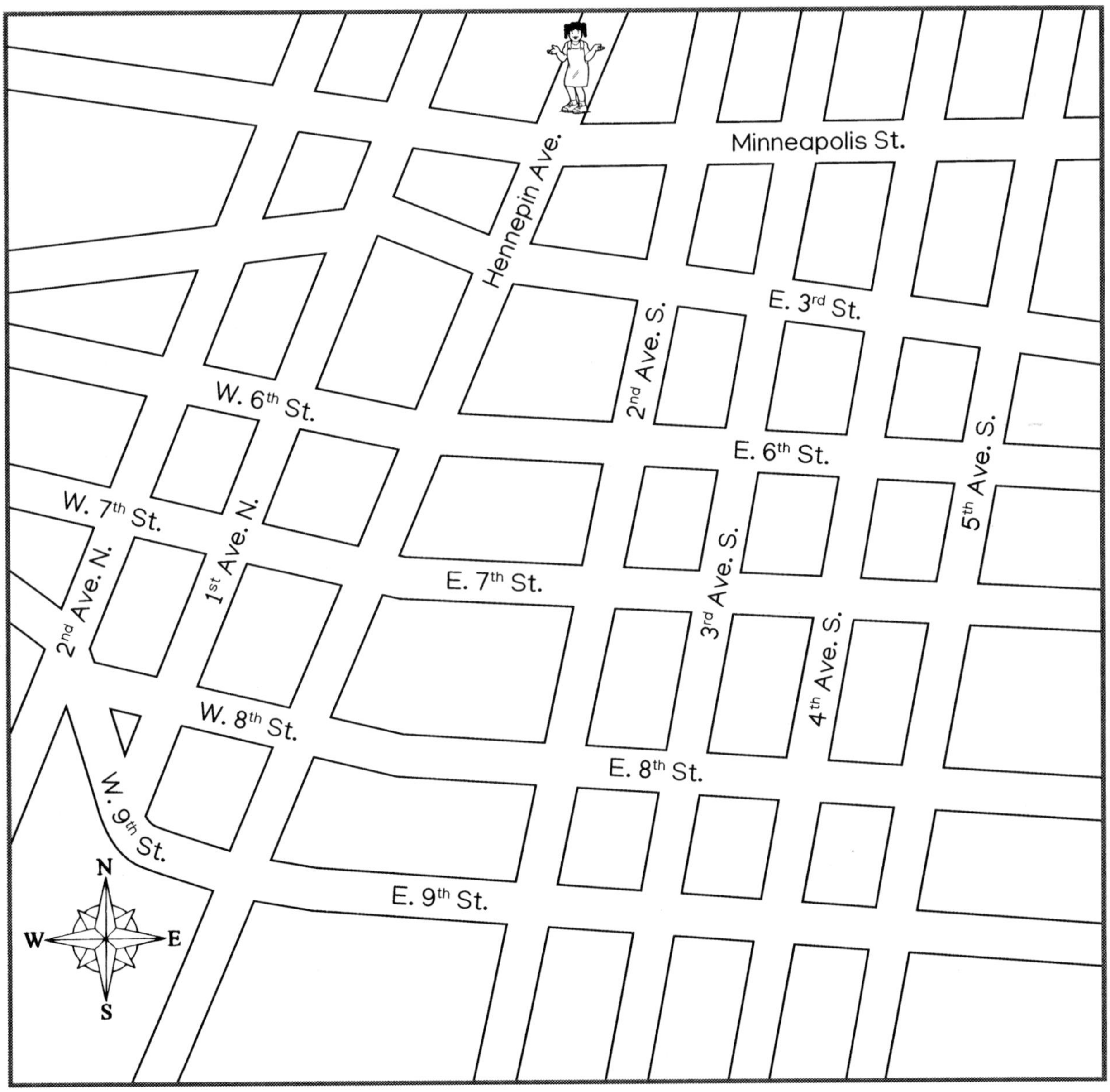

Multiples and Factors

Directions: Read each problem carefully. Circle the correct answer. *Hint:* LCM means Lowest Common Multiple, and GCF means Greatest Common Factor.

Instrucciones: Lee cada problema cuidadosamente. Haz un círculo alrededor de la respuesta correcta. *Sugerencia:* LCM significa el Minimo Múltiplo Común ("Lowest Common Multiple") y GCF significa el Máximo Común Divisor ("Greatest Common Factor").

Examples

A. Find the LCM of 5 and 12.
- a. 16
- (b.) 60
- c. 24
- d. 120

B. Find the GCF of 20 and 30.
- (a.) 10
- b. 20
- c. 1
- d. 2

1. Find the GCF of 8 and 40.
   - a. 10
   - b. 9
   - c. 8
   - d. none of the above

2. Find the LCM of 8 and 10.
   - a. 10
   - b. 40
   - c. 36
   - d. 80

3. Find the GCF of 12 and 27.
   - a. 4
   - b. 9
   - c. 6
   - d. 3

4. Find the LCM of 7 and 9.
   - a. 7
   - b. 9
   - c. 54
   - d. 63

5. Find the GCF of 48 and 36.
   - a. 9
   - b. 16
   - c. 12
   - d. none of the above

6. Find the GCF of 8 and 27.
   - a. 1
   - b. 4
   - c. 8
   - d. 7

7. Find the LCM of 3 and 15.
   - a. 15
   - b. 30
   - c. 12
   - d. 21

8. Find the LCM of 9 and 20.
   - a. 150
   - b. 160
   - c. 180
   - d. 20

Adverbs

What to Know **Adverbs** are words that describe verbs, adjectives, or other adverbs. They answer these questions: *When? To what extent? How?*

Examples: My father ran *yesterday. (When?)*
Maribelle sang *badly. (How?)*
She *partially* finished her homework. *(To what extent?)*

Most adverbs are formed by adding *–ly* to an adjective. Here are some examples:

Adjective	Adverb
soft	softly
sad	sadly
beautiful	beautifully
quick	quickly
mad	madly

Other adverbs do not end in *–ly*. Some examples are *already, often, far, now, more,* and *soon.*

Directions: Rewrite each sentence. Add adverbs to answer the questions in parentheses.

Instrucciones: Vuelve a escribir cada oración. Agrega adverbios para responder las palabras entre paréntesis.

1. The monkey did tricks for the crowd. *(When?)*

   ____

2. The teacher gave the instructions. *(How?)*

   ____

3. I ate my dinner. *(To what extent?)*

   ____

Directions: Add adverbs to the sentences below to correspond with the question after each sentence.

Instrucciones: Agrega adverbios a las oraciones para combinarlas con cada una de las preguntas que figuran después de cada oración.

4. I ______________________ understand your argument. *(To what extent?)*
5. We're moving to a new city ______________________. *(When?)*
6. My older brother sings ______________________ in the shower. *(How?)*
7. The tree fell ______________________. *(How?)*

Candy Fractions

Directions: Candy Is Dandy is a special candy store. Use your knowledge of fractions to help Candy Is Dandy serve its customers.

Instrucciones: "Candy Is Dandy" es una tienda de dulces especial. Usa tu conocimiento de las fracciones para ayudar a "Candy Is Dandy" a atender a sus clientes.

1. Your mother bought $\frac{1}{3}$ of a pound of Jelly Smellies and $\frac{1}{4}$ of a pound of Gooey Gummies. How many pounds of candy did she buy? __________

2. One teacher bought $\frac{3}{4}$ of a pound of Nutty Buddies, and another bought $\frac{2}{3}$ of a pound of Nutty Buddies. How many pounds did they buy in all? __________

3. Kel bought $\frac{7}{8}$ of a pound of Slurpy Suckers. Dex bought $\frac{3}{4}$ of a pound of Slurpy Suckers. How much more did Kel buy? __________

4. Coach Kim bought $\frac{11}{12}$ of a pound of Choco-Nuts, and Coach Lee bought $\frac{5}{6}$ of a pound. How much more did Coach Kim buy? __________

5. Chocolate Yums are sold in baggies that hold $\frac{1}{3}$ of a pound. Bob bought 15 bags of Chocolate Yums. How many pounds of candy did he buy? __________

6. Chris bought $\frac{3}{4}$ of a foot of Luscious Licorice. James only bought $\frac{1}{3}$ as much licorice as Chris. How much licorice did James buy? __________

7. Christine bought $\frac{9}{10}$ of a pound of Chocolate Yums and $\frac{4}{5}$ of a pound of Choco-Nuts. How much candy did she buy altogether? __________

8. Sarah bought $\frac{1}{8}$ of a foot of Luscious Licorice and Angela bought $\frac{7}{12}$ of a foot of Luscious Licorice. How much less did Sarah buy? __________

9. Ed bought $\frac{3}{4}$ of a pound of Chocolate Yums, which he split evenly into cups holding $\frac{1}{8}$ of a pound each. How many cups did he have? __________

10. Mo bought $\frac{1}{2}$ of a pound of Nutty Buddies, $\frac{4}{5}$ of a pound of Gooey Gummies, and $\frac{1}{3}$ of a pound of Slurpy Suckers. How many pounds of candy did he buy altogether? __________

Could You Do It?

Directions: Read the passage and answer the questions below.

Instrucciones: Lee el párrafo y responde las preguntas.

Written Without Ease

The novel *Gadsby* was written by Ernest Vincent Wright and published in 1939. It tells the story of its title character, an ambitious man named John Gadsby. He lives in a fictional American town called Branton Hills. This town is in bad shape, and Gadsby decides to do something about it. He becomes the mayor, and the town thrives.

That is the plot of *Gadsby*, but it is not what makes this novel really unique and ambitious. What makes *Gadsby* special is that it is written without the help of one very important thing: the letter *e*. There are over 50,000 words in *Gadsby*, and not one contains the letter *e*. This must have been difficult, since the letter *e* appears in about 12.5% of the words in the English language. It was so difficult, in fact, that Wright tied down the letter *e* on his typewriter so that "none of that vowel might slip in, accidentally."

1. What is not true of John Gadsby? Circle one answer.
   - a. He is the author of *Gadsby*.
   - b. He is the title character of *Gadsby*.
   - c. He is the mayor of Branton Hills.
   - d. There are no *e*s in his name.

2. Which of these sentences could be in the novel *Gadsby*? Circle all correct answers.
   - a. A burglar was caught with stolen goods.
   - b. Two cats scratch at an old shop sign.
   - c. It was his last chance to catch a bus to town.
   - d. A rising sun signals morning's arrival.

3. Can you write a paragraph of at least 3 sentences without using one letter? Give it a try. Choose one of the vowels and cross it out. Write a paragraph that does not contain that letter. Your paragraph can be about any subject you choose.

   a e i o u

Table Read

Directions: The table to the left shows the frequency with which each letter appears in words in the English language. Each percentage has been rounded to the nearest 0.5% (except for letters appearing in fewer than 0.5% of words). Use this table to answer the questions, either by circling the letter of the correct answer or by writing the correct answer on the line provided.

Instrucciones: La tabla de la izquierda muestra la frecuencia con la que aparece cada letra en las palabras en el idioma inglés. Cada porcentaje ha sido redondeado al 0,5% más cercano (excepto para letras que aparecen en menos del 0,5% de las palabras). Usa esta tabla para responder las preguntas, ya sea haciendo un círculo alrededor de la letra de la respuesta correcta o escribiendo la respuesta correcta en la línea provista.

Most Common Letters in English	
A	8%
B	1.5%
C	3%
D	4.5%
E	12.5%
F	2%
G	2%
H	6%
I	7%
J	.15%
K	1%
L	4%
M	2.5%
N	6.5%
O	7.5%
P	2%
Q	.09%
R	6%
S	6.5%
T	9%
U	3%
V	1%
W	2.5%
X	.15%
Y	2%
Z	.07%

1. According to the table, what are the five most common letters in the English language? The correct answer shows these letters in order from most common to least common.

   a. e, a, i, o, u **b.** e, t, s, a, i **c.** e, t, a, o, i **d.** e, a, t, i, o

2. What is the difference in percentage between the most common letter and the fifth most common letter?

   a. 5% **b.** 4.5% **c.** 4% **d.** 5.5%

3. If a paragraph contains 200 words, how many of those words would you expect to contain the letter *a*?

   a. 80 **b.** 16 **c.** 50 **d.** 8

   How did you come up with your answer? ____________________

   ____

4. Look at this word: *pencil*. Write the letters in order from most common to least common.

   ____

5. Think about the word *baseball* and about how many times each of its letters appears in the word. What percentage of the word *baseball* does each letter represent?

   a ________ b ________ e ________ l ________ s ________

   Label the pie chart to represent the frequencies of the letters *a*, *b*, *e*, *l*, and *s* in the word *baseball*.

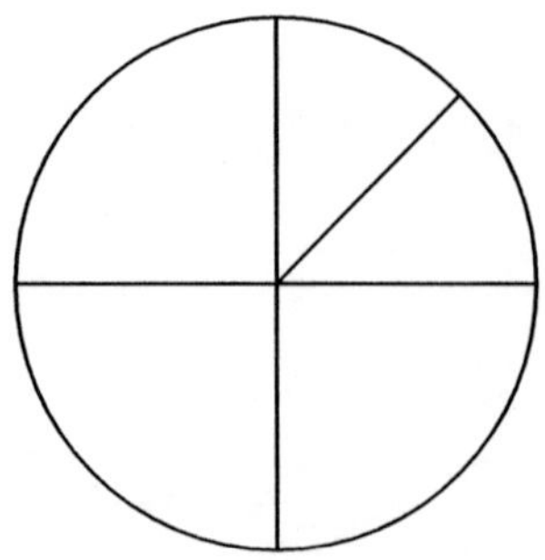

Commas in a Series

What to Know

Use a comma to separate three or more words in a series. The comma goes between words in a series. The "and" goes between the second to last word and the last word in the series.

Examples: Manatees are slow, gentle, and curious creatures.

Directions: Use each set of words in a sentence. When appropriate, add commas and the word "and."

Instrucciones: Usa cada conjunto de palabras en una oración. Cuando sea apropiado, agrega comas y la palabra "and".

1. scissors paper glue

 ____

 ____

2. grass weeds kelp

 ____

 ____

3. warm calm shallow

 ____

 ____

4. United States Canada Mexico

 ____

 ____

5. lemons limes oranges

 ____

 ____

6. scratched cat bruised

 ____

 ____

Math Mix

Part I Directions: Some states require that out-of-state businesses pay a shipping tax to send goods to state residents. Refer to this table to solve the problems below. (*Note:* The shipping rates do not reflect the actual current rates.)

Parte I Instrucciones: Algunos estados exigen que las empresas de otros estados paguen un impuesto de envío para enviar mercancías a los residentes del estado. Consulta esta tabla para resolver los siguientes problemas. (*Nota:* Las tasas no reflejan las tasas actuales reales).

Shipping Taxes

State	Abbr.	Rate	State	Abbr.	Rate
Alabama	AL	8.00%	Indiana	IN	5.00%
Maryland	MD	5.75%	Kentucky	KY	6.00%
Georgia	GA	4.00%	Missouri	MO	5.725%
Illinois	IL	2.00%			

1. Miguel lives in Maryland and purchased a sweater for $39.99 from a catalog. Add the shipping tax. What's the total cost of the sweater?

   ____

2. The Wongs paid a total of $200.00 for a television for their home in Illinois. The salesperson said that a 2% shipping tax was already added to the final price. What was the price of the television before the tax was added? Circle your answer.

   a. $202.00 b. $198.00 c. $196.08 d. $198.06

3. The Wood family lives in Lexington, KY. They purchased a computer for $1,295.00. What is the total price for the computer after the shipping tax is added?

   ____

Part II Directions: Complete the table below. Find the fraction, decimal, and/or percent equivalent to the one given. Write each fraction in lowest terms.

Parte II Instrucciones: Completa la siguiente tabla. Encuentra el equivalente en fracciones, decimales y/o porcentajes al ejemplo dado. Escribe cada fracción en términos mínimos.

	Fraction	Decimal	Percent
1.	$\frac{1}{10}$		
2.		.25	
3.			45%
4.			15%
5.	$\frac{4}{5}$		

Works of Art

What to Know Use quotation marks in writing titles of short works, such as magazine articles, short stories, poems, songs, and chapters of books.

Part I Directions: Read the following paragraph. Insert quotation marks wherever needed.

Parte I Instrucciones: Lee el siguiente párrafo. Inserta comillas donde sea necesario.

My favorite poem, Love Is Alive, was written by American poet Sophie Harrington. I read anything written by or about her that I can find. I was especially happy to find that, in my subscription to *Grandeur*, there was an article entitled Up and Coming Poets that featured Sophie and her work. As I read the article, I was surprised to discover that she has also written several short stories. Her latest short story, The How and Why of It All, is scheduled to be in the next issue of *Grandeur*. Since I too am a writer, she has inspired me to begin writing a song that I've tentatively titled, My Inspiration. I may even send her a copy of it, once I have it completed.

What to Know Use underlining or *italics* for titles of longer works, such as books, TV shows, movies, works of art, and the names of ships.

Part II Directions: Write two sentences. Each must include the name of a work of art. Choose from the categories in the box. Remember to underline the title of each work of art.

Parte II Instrucciones: Escribe dos oraciones. Cada una debe incluir el nombre de una obra de arte. Escoge de las categorías brindadas en el recuadro. Recuerda subrayar el título de cada obra de arte.

novel	film	TV show	comic book	video game

1. ____

____

2. ____

____

O.I.C.

Directions: Each box below contains a common word or phrase. Study each box until you say, "Oh, I see!" Once you've uncovered the word or phrase, write it on the line.

Instrucciones: Cada cuadro a continuación contiene una palabra o frase común. Estudia cada caja hasta que digas, "Oh, I see!" Una vez que haya descubierto la palabra o frase, escríbela en la línea.

lang4uage

1. ______________________

2. ______________________

YOUR	THEIR
 M	

3. ______________________

dice dice

4. ______________________

k
c
e
h
c

5. ______________________

O dom

6. ______________________

Go *it it it it*

7. ______________________

sitting
THE WORLD

8. ______________________

mi1llion

9. ______________________

The Missing Link

Directions: Each problem gives you three words that don't seem related. Can you find the missing link that connects the three words? An example is done for you.

Instrucciones: Cada problema te da tres palabras que no parecen relacionadas. ¿Puedes encontrar el eslabón perdido que conecta las tres palabras? Un ejemplo está hecho para ti.

1.	garbage	soda	soup	can
2.	dinosaur	Easter	scrambled	
3.	whipped	sour	cheese	
4.	trash	pipes	shopping	
5.	moon	night	year	
6.	tree	core	pie	
7.	play	pig	pal	
8.	sea	race	shoe	
9.	ball	lash	lid	
10.	back	jet	wolf	
11.	fly	camp	fighter	
12.	way	ball	plane	

Single Bar Graphs

Directions: This single bar graph shows the number of electoral votes for each of the 10 most-populated states. There are 538 electoral votes distributed among the 50 states and the District of Columbia. It takes 270 electoral votes to win a presidential election. Use the information on the graph to answer the questions below.

Instrucciones: Este gráfico de barra única muestra el número de votos electorales para cada uno de los 10 estados más poblados. Hay 538 votos electorales repartidos entre los 50 estados y el Distrito de Columbia. Se necesitan 270 votos electorales para ganar una elección presidencial. Utiliza el información en el gráfico para responder las siguientes preguntas.

1. How many electoral votes does California have?

2. How many electoral votes does Texas have?

3. What is the interval between numbers on the scale?

4. How many electoral votes does North Carolina have?

5. What is the difference in the number of votes between Michigan and Illinois?

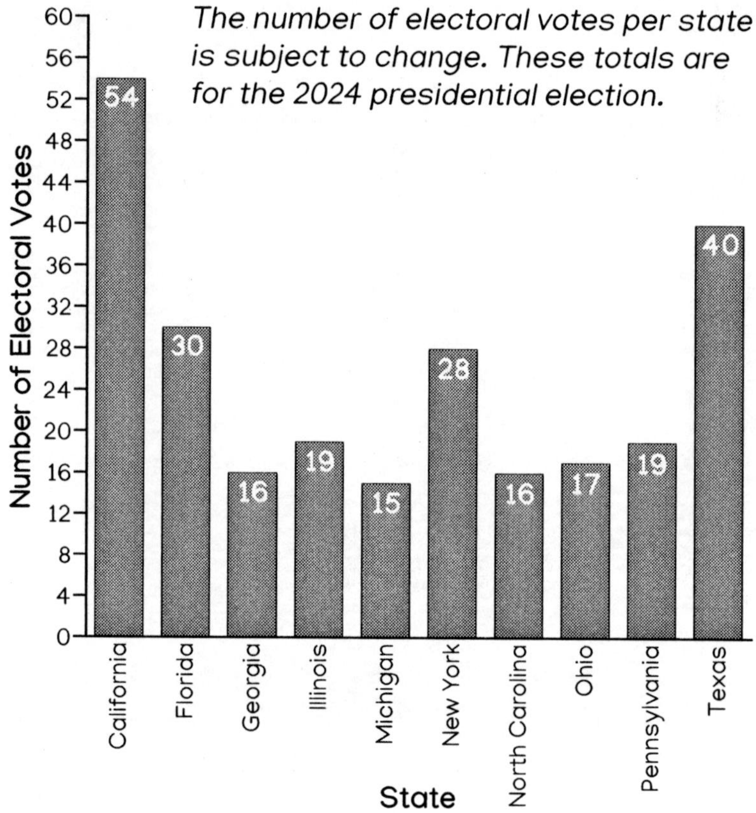

The number of electoral votes per state is subject to change. These totals are for the 2024 presidential election.

6. Which state has exactly 12 fewer electoral votes than Texas?

7. What is the total number of electoral votes of these 10 states?

8. How many electoral votes are distributed among the remaining 40 states and the District of Columbia?

9. Why would a candidate spend more time campaigning in Florida than in Ohio?

10. If a candidate won these 10 states, how many more electoral votes would they need to win a presidential election?

The Best Definition

Directions: For each sentence below, choose the definition that matches the way the underlined word is used in the sentence. Circle the letter beside each correct answer.

Instrucciones: Para cada oración, elige la definición que coincida con la forma en que la palabra subrayada se usa en la oración. Encierra en un círculo la letra junto a cada respuesta correcta.

1. The senator proposed a bill to ban the use of the toxic chemical.
   a. amount of money owed for a service
   b. the visor part of a cap
   c. text of a law presented for discussion
2. The phone bill included a slight charge for upgrading to a new network.
   a. money expected for a service or good
   b. electrical power restored to a device
   c. guilt or blame placed for the committing of a crime
3. The referee separated the two players once their argument became heated.
   a. warmed, as in a vehicle or building
   b. intensified, as in an emotion
   c. warmed, as in a solid or liquid
4. One by one, the students began to file in to the classroom and take their seats.
   a. march in a line
   b. use a tool to smooth or reduce
   c. put something in a place where it can be retrieved at a later date
5. To make a model of the planets to scale, we cleared a large area on the school's field.
   a. to climb up to or over the top of a tall object
   b. the relation between the real size of something and its size in a representation of it
   c. a flat plate-like part on a reptile, fish, or other animal
6. After 40 minutes, the annoyed judge asked, "What is the point of this story?"
   a. a particular place or moment in time
   b. the sharp end of something
   c. the main idea or reason for something
7. During the summer, her sweaters were kept in the trunk at the foot of her bed.
   a. the main stem of a tree
   b. a spacious compartment in a vehicle
   c. a sturdy box for holding things
8. Before 1900, the town did not keep a record of local weather events.
   a. the highest or best accomplishment of something
   b. an account in writing intended to preserve information
   c. something on which sound has been stored so that it can be played back

Double Bar Graphs

Directions: This double bar graph illustrates a survey about participant sports for boys in the third through the eighth grades.

Instrucciones: Este gráfico de barras dobles ilustra una encuesta sobre deportes participantes para niños de tercero a octavo grado.

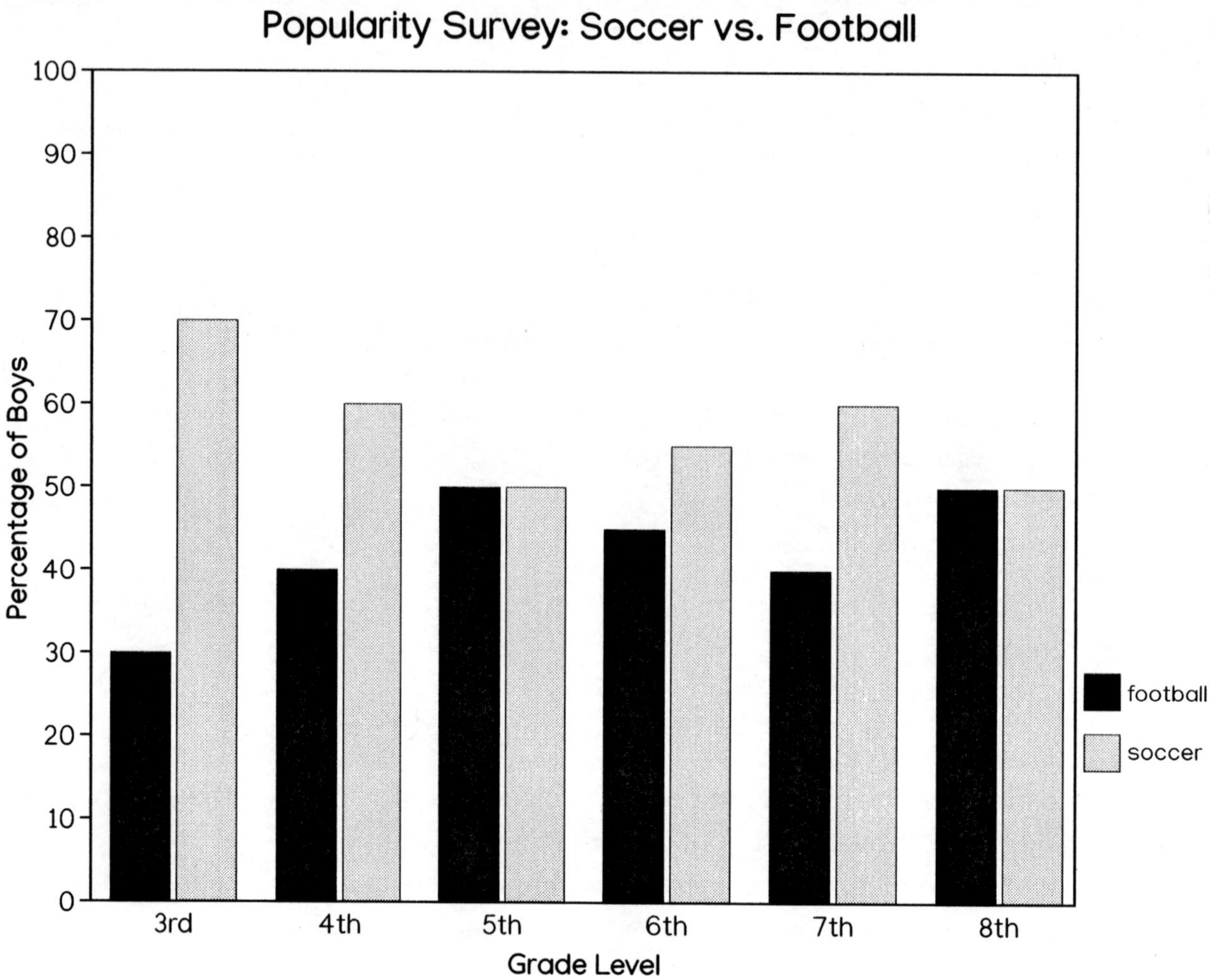

1. What percentage of third-grade boys preferred to play football? ____________
2. In which two grades do boys like to play soccer and football equally well? ____________
3. What percentage of boys in the fourth grade prefer soccer? ____________
4. What percentage of boys prefer football in the sixth grade? ____________
5. What percentage of boys prefer football in the seventh grade? ____________
6. Does this type of graph help you make comparisons? Explain your answer.

____

____

Prepositions

What to Know

Prepositions are words that show a relationship between other words.

To see how prepositions work, look at the words *fox* and *log*. Prepositions can show the relationship between the *fox* and the *log*:

The fox was *under* the log. The fox was *on* the log.

The fox was *by* the log. The fox was *in* the log.

In these examples, the word *fox* is the subject of the sentence, and the word *log* is the object of the preposition.

Prepositions always start prepositional phrases. A phrase is a group of words that doesn't make a whole sentence. The following are all prepositional phrases: *under the log, on the log, by the log, in the log.*

Part I Directions: Write the prepositional phrase from each sentence on the line. Circle the object of the preposition and underline the preposition.

Parte I Instrucciones: Escribe la frase preposicional de cada oración en la línea. Encierra en un círculo el objeto de la preposición y subráyala.

1. Penguins live at the South Pole.
   ____
2. The students slept during the speech.
   ____
3. The fish in the pan smelled awful.
   ____
4. The announcer on TV was excited.
   ____
5. I found the keys under the table.
   ____
6. We are going to the movies tomorrow.
   ____
7. The rabbit hopped across the road.
   ____
8. The girls climbed to the top.
   ____

Part II Directions: Rewrite each sentence. Add a prepositional phrase.

Parte II Instrucciones: Vuelve a escribir cada oración. Añadir una frase preposicional.

1. The dog ate his dinner. The dog ate his dinner by the back door.
2. The boys ran. ______________________
   ____
3. Josh did his work. ______________________
   ____

Averages

What to Know

To compute an average:

- Add all of the separate values in a set of data.
- Divide by the number of values of data.

Directions: Students in a sixth-grade classroom collected data by surveying classmates on a variety of subjects. Help them compute the average for each topic. Round each answer to the nearest hundredth.

Instrucciones: Los estudiantes de un salón de clases de sexto grado recopilaron datos encuestando a sus compañeros de clase en una variedad de temas. Ayúdalos a calcular el promedio de cada tema. Redondea cada respuesta a la centésima más cercana.

1. A group of 9 boys in the classroom were measured for height. These were the heights recorded in inches: 51, 61, 57, 63, 60, 59, 60, 55, 62.

   Total: ________ Divided by: ________ Average: ________

2. A group of 11 students recorded these math scores: 88, 56, 92, 96, 100, 87, 66, 75, 81, 80, 90.

   Total: ________ Divided by: ________ Average: ________

3. These were the weights in pounds of 13 students surveyed: 88, 84, 77, 78, 90, 100, 106, 95, 96, 84, 88, 93, 81.

   Total: ________ Divided by: ________ Average: ________

4. A group of 10 students sold Valentine candy boxes during a school fundraising project. These were the number of boxes sold: 14, 20, 12, 8, 6, 3, 15, 19, 24, 17.

   Total: ________ Divided by: ________ Average: ________

5. Thirteen students were surveyed on the number of hours they spent watching television in one week. These were the responses: 20, 23, 14, 7, 6, 1, 0, 15, 30, 20, 12, 8, 19.

   Total: ________ Divided by: ________ Average: ________

6. Sixteen students surveyed listed the number of hours they spent exercising each week: 10, 9, 12, 4, 5, 1, 2, 8, 9, 5, 3, 2, 15, 14, 5, 3.

   Total: ________ Divided by: ________ Average: ________

The Apology

Directions: This passage is an excerpt from the book *Do They Play Marbles on Mars?* by Margaret McAlister. Read the passage, then answer the questions below.

Instrucciones: Este párrafo es un resumen de un libro llamado *Do They Play Marbles on Mars?* escrito por Margaret McAlister. Lee el párrafo, luego responde las preguntas a continuación.

"I saw that, Michael!" said Mrs. Jackson. "Come out here!"

"What?" I tried to look innocent. "What did I do?"

Mrs. Jackson sighed. She looked up at the ceiling then back at me.

"Apologize to Cheryl."

Now, that was really heavy. It was only a bit of crumpled paper. Nobody ever died from being hit on the head by an old math test.

Cheryl smirked. I glared at her. Cheryl had done much worse things to me. Mrs. Jackson hardly ever caught her. I should have just told Mrs. Jackson that Cheryl put a matchbox full of loose ants in my lunch box.

"Go ahead, Michael," said Mrs. Jackson. "Unless you'd like to pick up papers for a week."

I thought about it for a moment. It would almost be worth it to choose the papers, but then I thought of Cheryl following me around all week yelling insults while I picked up the trash. Then I would be forced to stuff some dirty, sticky wrappers down her T-shirt . . . and then I would get two weeks of picking up papers . . .

"Sorry," I muttered, looking at the floor.

1. Mrs. Jackson is most likely
   a. Cheryl's mother.
   b. Michael's mother.
   c. a teacher.
   d. a cleaner.

2. Michael said he was sorry because
   a. Cheryl had been really hurt.
   b. he hadn't meant to be nasty.
   c. it was better than picking up papers.
   d. he had been in the wrong and knew it.

3. How well did Michael and Cheryl get along? Explain your answer. ____________________

____

____

4. Why did Michael look at the floor when he apologized? ____________________

____

____

5. The word *smirk* means to smile in what manner?
   a. happily
   b. meanly
   c. sweetly
   d. sadly

Mean, Median, Mode

What to Know

- The **mean** of a set of numbers is the average. To find the mean, add up the total of all the given values and divide by the total number of values.

  10 12 12 4 7 → 10 + 12 + 12 + 4 + 7 = 45 ÷ 5 = 9 **mean** = 9

- The **median** of a set of numbers is the middle value. Put the numbers in order from least to greatest and find the number that comes in the middle. If there are two numbers in the middle, find the average of those two numbers.

  10 12 12 4 7 → 4 7 (10) 12 12 **median** = 10

- The **mode** of a set of numbers is the number that occurs most frequently. Some sets of numbers have more than one mode. Some do not have a mode.

  10 12 12 4 7 → 4 7 10 (12 12) **mode** = 12

Directions: Sixth-graders read books as part of their reading program. The number of books each class read in one week was totaled and graphed below. Use this graph to answer the questions below.

Instrucciones: Los estudiantes de sexto grado leen libros como parte de su programa de lectura. La cantidad de libros leídos en cada clase en una semana fue totalizada y graficada a continuación. Usa este gráfico para responder preguntas.

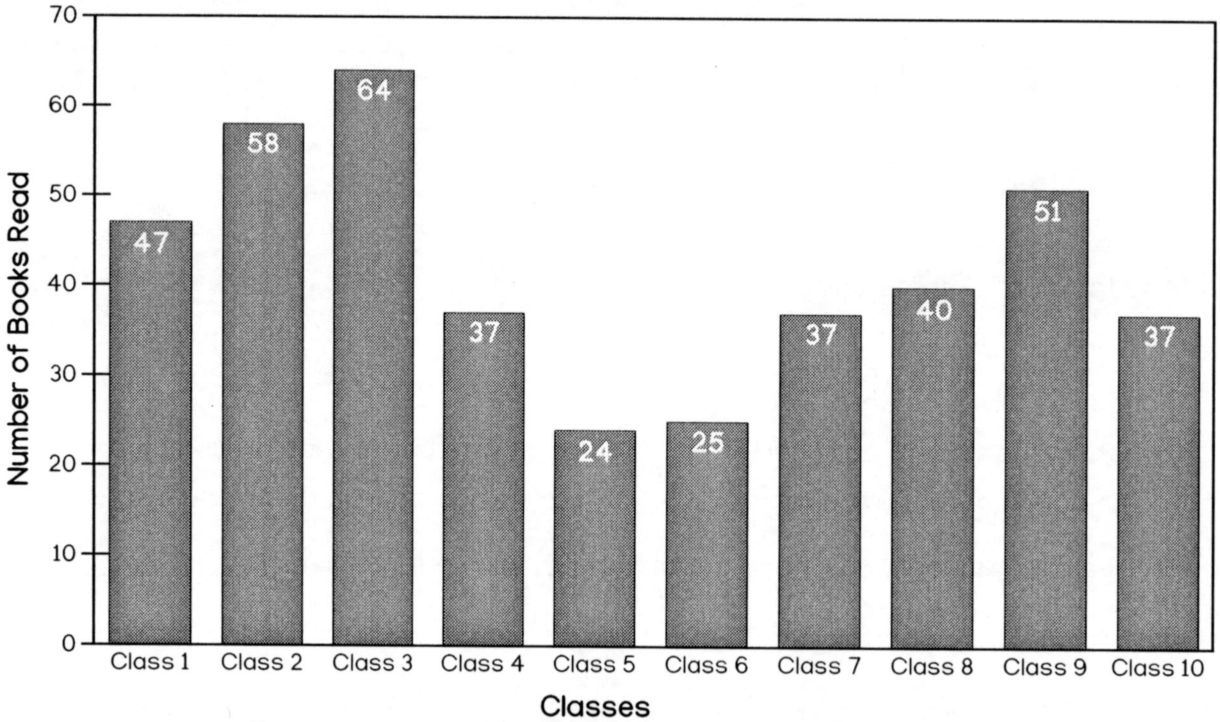

1. What is the mode number of books read by all the classes? ____________
2. What is the median number of books read by all the classes? ____________
3. What is the mean number of books read by all of the classes? ____________

Thirteen Sentences

Directions: Use the following words to create 14 sentences. You can change the forms of the words (for example, tense, singular to plural) and add extra words as needed. Try to use one word from each list in each sentence. Do not use any word twice.

Instrucciones: Usa las siguientes palabras para crear 14 oraciones. Puedes cambiar las formas de la palabras (por ejemplo, tiempo, singular a plural) y agrega palabras adicionales según sea necesario. Intenta usar una palabra de cada lista en cada oración. No utilices ninguna palabra dos veces.

Nouns	Verbs	Adjectives	Adverbs	Prepositions
scientist	shout	sad	quietly	into
squirrel	sniff	chilly	energetically	before
football	giggle	complicated	dismally	after
palm tree	consider	green	respectfully	until
asphalt	ski	enormous	yesterday	in
George	fly	miniscule	loudly	through
kangaroo	stare	sweet	happily	around
macaroni	shriek	confused	urgently	below
girl	dance	awkward	seriously	inside
ice cube	try	sleepy	encouragingly	during
broccoli	jump	pink	messily	under
sunflower	roar	silent	softly	on
cat	hop	sticky	sloppily	above

1. ______________________________

2. ______________________________

3. ______________________________

4. ______________________________

5. ______________________________

6. ______________________________

7. ______________________________

8. ______________________________

9. ______________________________

10. ______________________________

11. ______________________________

12. ______________________________

13. ______________________________

DIY Dinner Club

Directions: The DIY Dinner Club is held every Friday night at 6:30. Find the time each member arrived and the food item each brought. If the answer is "yes," make an O in the box. If the answer is "no," make an X in the box.

Instrucciones: El "DIY Dinner Club" se lleva a cabo todos los viernes por la noche a las 6:30. Encuentre la hora en que llegó cada miembro y la comida que trajo cada uno. Si la respuesta es "sí," haz una O en el recuadro. Si la respuesta es "no", marca con una X en la casilla.

Clues

- Roland was late for the DIY Dinner.
- Betty arrived after Charice.
- Paul arrived before the person who brought the spaghetti.
- Charice's rolls were still warm when she arrived.
- Heidi arrived right on time.
- Paul didn't bring the salad or the sodas.
- Betty brought the spaghetti, and Heidi brought the salad.
- Betty arrived at 6:15, and Paul arrived before Charice.

	5:45	6:00	6:15	6:30	6:45	Dessert	Rolls	Salad	Sodas	Spaghetti
Betty										
Charice										
Heidi										
Paul										
Roland										

1. Betty arrived at ____________________ and brought the ____________________.
2. Charice arrived at ____________________ and brought the ____________________.
3. Heidi arrived at ____________________ and brought the ____________________.
4. Paul arrived at ____________________ and brought the ____________________.
5. Roland arrived at ____________________ and brought the ____________________.

Droodles

What to Know

Droodles are artistic interpretations of brainteasers. Pictures or illustrations are used to present information. Symbols may represent different things depending on the context. Word clues may be added.

Directions: What could these droodles be? Write your answers on the lines.

Instrucciones: ¿Qué podrían ser estos garabatos? Escribe tus respuestas en las líneas.

Droodle #1

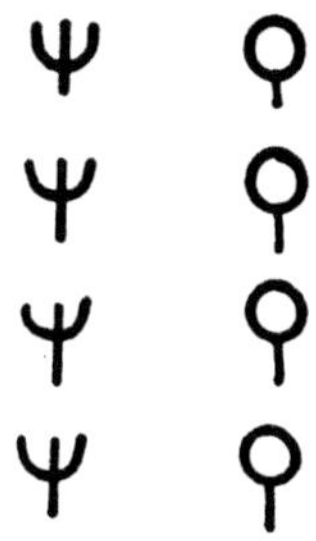

What could it be? ______________________

____

Droodle #2

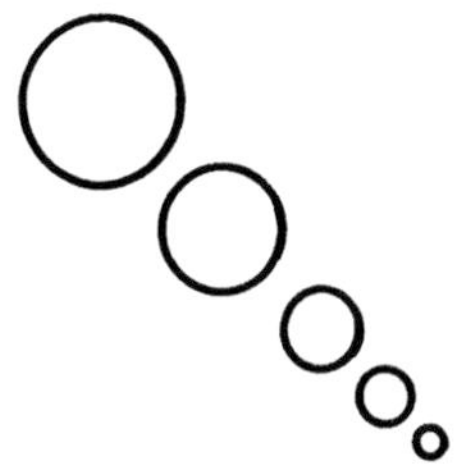

What could it be? ______________________

____

Droodle #3

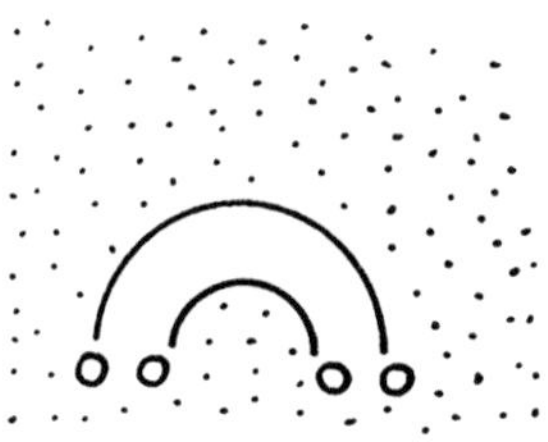

What could it be? ______________________

____

Droodle #4

What could it be? ______________________

____

Droodle #5

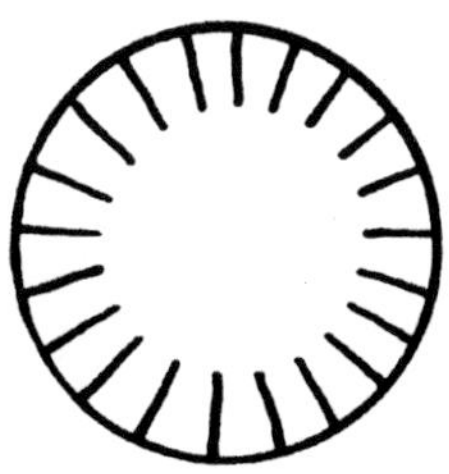

What could it be? ______________________

____

Droodle #6

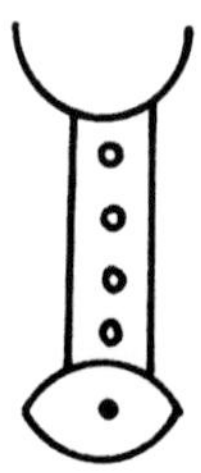

What could it be? ______________________

____

Square Roots

What to Know

The **square root** of a number is another number that multiplied by itself will equal the first number.

The square root of 9 is 3 because $3 \times 3 = 9$. This radical symbol $\sqrt{\ }$ indicates that you need to find the square root.

$\sqrt{25} = 5$ $\sqrt{36} = 6$

Directions: Use the information and examples above to help solve these problems. Use a calculator to help you check the answers on the more difficult problems.

Instrucciones: Usa la información y los ejemplos anteriores para ayudar a resolver estos problemas. Utiliza una calculadora para ayudarte a comprobar las respuestas de los problemas más difíciles.

1. $\sqrt{4}$ = ________
2. $\sqrt{16}$ = ________
3. $\sqrt{49}$ = ________
4. $\sqrt{81}$ = ________
5. $\sqrt{100}$ = ________
6. $\sqrt{64}$ = ________
7. $\sqrt{121}$ = ________
8. $\sqrt{144}$ = ________
9. $\sqrt{169}$ = ________
10. $\sqrt{225}$ = ________
11. $\sqrt{196}$ = ________
12. $\sqrt{400}$ = ________
13. $\sqrt{900}$ = ________
14. $\sqrt{4,900}$ = ________
15. $\sqrt{6,400}$ = ________
16. $\sqrt{1,600}$ = ________
17. $\sqrt{490,000}$ = ________
18. $\sqrt{640,000}$ = ________
19. $\sqrt{160,000}$ = ________
20. $\sqrt{810,000}$ = ________
21. $\sqrt{250,000}$ = ________
22. $\sqrt{90,000}$ = ________
23. $\sqrt{360,000}$ = ________
24. $\sqrt{10,000}$ = ________

Greek Mythology

Directions: Read the passage, then answer the questions below using complete sentences.

Instrucciones: Lee el pasaje, luego responde las preguntas usando oraciones completas.

The Myth of Narcissus

Zeus, the supreme god, persuaded Echo to distract his wife, Hera, by chattering incessantly. He did this so that Hera could not keep track of him, leaving him free to be around other women. However, when Hera figured out the plan, she was so enraged that she took away Echo's voice, leaving her with only the ability to repeat the final word of every message she heard. When Echo saw the extremely handsome but vain Narcissus, she fell deeply in love with him. Of course, she could not tell him of her love, but she followed him everywhere, gazing at him lovingly until he haughtily rejected her. Poor Echo hid in a cave and wasted away until only her voice remained. Then, the goddess Nemesis decided to punish Narcissus by making him fall hopelessly in love with his own face as he saw it reflected in a pool. He gazed in fascination, unable to tear himself away from his image, until he gradually wasted away. In the spot where he had sat grew a beautiful yellow flower, which even to this day bears the name *narcissus*.

1. What did Zeus ask Echo to do? ______________________________

____

2. Why did he ask her to do this? ______________________________

____

3. What was Hera's reaction? ______________________________

____

4. Why did Echo fall in love with Narcissus? ______________________________

____

5. What was Narcissus's reaction to Echo? ______________________________

____

6. What did Nemesis do to Narcissus? ______________________________

____

7. What happened to Echo in the end? ______________________________

____

8. What happened to Narcissus in the end? ______________________________

____

Ratios

Directions: Discount Sports has thousands of items to appeal to every interest. Help the owners compute these ratios. Use the illustrations. The first one has been done for you.

Instrucciones: "Discount Sports" tiene miles de artículos para atraer a todos los intereses. Ayuda a los dueños a calcular estas proporciones. Usa las ilustraciones. El ejemplo es para ti.

Balls	
Bats	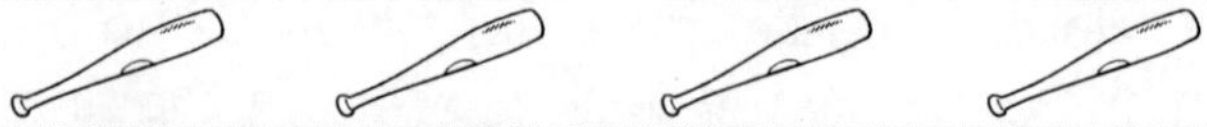
Mitts	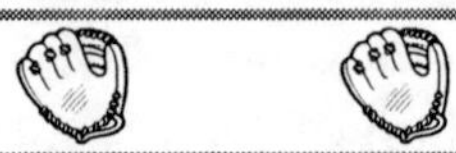
Shoes	

1. What is the ratio of balls to bats? 5:4 or 5/4
2. What is the ratio of bats to balls? ______________
3. What is the ratio of mitts to balls? ______________
4. What is the ratio of balls to mitts? ______________
5. What is the ratio of shoes to balls? ______________
6. What is the ratio of balls to shoes? ______________
7. What is the ratio of bats to shoes? ______________
8. What is the ratio of shoes to bats? ______________

Bicycles	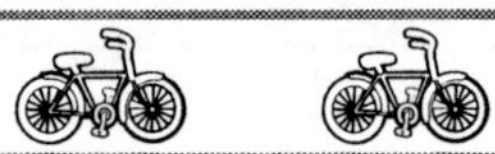
Kites	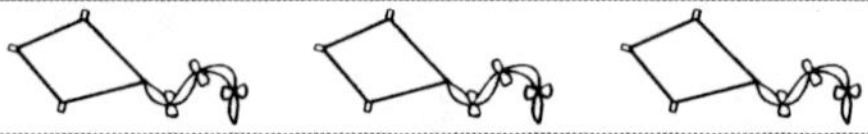
Soccer Balls	
Skateboards	

9. What is the ratio of bicycles to kites? ______________
10. What is the ratio of kites to bicycles? ______________
11. What is the ratio of skateboards to soccer balls? ______________
12. What is the ratio of soccer balls to skateboards? ______________
13. What is the ratio of kites to skateboards? ______________
14. What is the ratio of skateboards to kites? ______________

Sentence Combining

Directions: Read both sentences. Circle the answer that shows the best way in which to combine them to make one sentence.

Instrucciones: Lee ambas oraciones. Encierra en un círculo la respuesta que muestre la mejor manera de combinarlas para hacer una oración.

Example

The flag is red, white, and blue. The flag has fifty stars.

a. The red, white, and blue flag 50 stars has.

b. Fifty stars the red, white, and blue flag has.

(c.) The red, white, and blue flag has fifty stars.

1. The dog is black. The dog has white patches.
   a. The dog is black, and the dog has white patches.
   b. The dog is black and has white patches.
   c. White patches the black dog has.

2. It is hot today. It is humid today.
   a. It is hot and humid today.
   b. Hot and humid it is today.
   c. Today, it is hot and it is humid.

3. Jason won the foot race. Jason hurt his leg while winning the foot race.
   a. Jason won the foot race and hurt his leg while winning the foot race.
   b. The foot race Jason won while hurting his leg.
   c. Jason won the foot race but hurt his leg.

4. Yesterday, I went to the mall. I bought two books and a pair of sandals.
   a. Yesterday, I went to the mall and bought two books and a pair of sandals.
   b. Two books and a pair of sandals I bought at the mall yesterday.
   c. At the mall yesterday, I went and bought two books and a pair of sandals.

5. I have to study for my social studies test. I have to do ten math problems.
   a. Ten math problems and study for my social studies test I have to.
   b. I have to study for my social studies test, and then I have to do ten math problems.
   c. I have to study for my social studies test and do ten math problems.

Rate Problems

What to Know

- To determine the rate of speed, divide the distance traveled by the time it took to travel that distance.
- The formula is: $r = \frac{d}{t}$
- The answer is usually expressed in miles per hour (m.p.h.).

Directions: Use the formula to determine each rate of speed.

Instrucciones: Usa la fórmula para determinar cada tasa de velocidad.

1. Your family took a 360-mile automobile trip from Los Angeles to San Francisco in 6 hours.

   What was your average speed? _______________ m.p.h.

2. The Clark family drove 3,000 miles from New York to Los Angeles in 60 hours.

   What was their average rate? _______________ m.p.h.

3. The Brown family traveled 990 miles from Atlanta, GA, to Houston, TX, in 33 hours.

   What was their average rate of speed? _______________ m.p.h.

4. Mark's mother drove 2,340 miles from Cincinnati, OH, to Portland, OR, in 39 hours.

   What was her average rate of speed? _______________ m.p.h.

5. Shannon's father drove 2,750 miles from Seattle, WA, to Philadelphia, PA, in 55 hours.

   What was his average speed? _______________ m.p.h.

6. Michelle's family drove 2,200 miles from Houston, TX, to Portland, OR, in 40 hours.

   What was their average rate of speed? _______________ m.p.h.

7. Alyssa's family drove 3,060 miles from San Francisco, CA, to Boston, MA, in 60 hours.

   What was their average speed? _______________ m.p.h.

8. Frank's dad drove 1,600 miles from Minneapolis, MN, to Seattle, WA, in 40 hours.

   What was his average speed? _______________ m.p.h.

9. Stacy's mother drove 1,040 miles from Denver, CO, to Memphis, TN, in 26 hours.

   What was her average speed? _______________ m.p.h.

10. Jake's dad flew a plane 195 miles from Kansas City, MO, to Omaha, NE, in 1.5 hours.

    What was the plane's average speed? _______________ m.p.h.

People Poetry

Part I Directions: Phrase poetry can describe an item or person without using complete sentences. Write a phrase poem using the example poem as a guide. End your phrase poem with a word that describes the subject of the poem.

Parte I Instrucciones: La poesía de frases puede describir un elemento o una persona sin usar oraciones completas. Escribe un poema de frase utilizando el ejemplo de poema como guía. Termina tu poema con una palabra que describa el tema del poema.

Morgan
rides a bike
loves spaghetti
chats on the phone
kicks the soccer ball
loves babies
Alive!

Subject: ______________________

Phrase 1: ______________________

Phrase 2: ______________________

Phrase 3: ______________________

Phrase 4: ______________________

Phrase 5: ______________________

One Word: ______________________

Part II Directions: Fill in the blanks below and you will have a poem about the person you know best—you!

Parte II Instrucciones: Completa los espacios en blanco a continuación y tendrás un poema sobre la persona que mejor conoces—tú!

I am ______________________

And ______________________

But I am not ______________________

I like ______________________

And ______________________

But I don't like ______________________

I feel ______________________

But I don't feel ______________________

Finding the Rate

Directions: *Rate* tells the measure of one quantity as it relates to the value of another quantity. Find the rate. Round to the nearest hundredth if your answer is not a whole number. The first one has been done for you.

Instrucciones: La *tasa* indica la medida de una cantidad en relación con el valor de otra cantidad. Encuentra la tasa. Redondea a la centésima más cercana si tu respuesta no es un número entero. Un ejemplo ha sido hecho para ti.

1. Bill can walk 3 miles in 45 minutes. How long will it take Bill to walk 10 miles? $\frac{\overset{1}{\cancel{3}} \text{ miles}}{\underset{15}{\cancel{45}} \text{ min.}} = \frac{10 \text{ miles}}{n}$ It will take Bill 150 minutes to walk 10 miles.	**2.** Marcie can jog a mile every 6 minutes. How many miles can Marcie jog in 30 minutes? Marcie can jog ________ miles in 30 minutes.
3. Andrew can skate 1 block every 15 seconds. How many blocks can Andrew skate in 2 minutes? Andrew can skate ________ blocks in 2 minutes.	**4.** Mona drove 40 miles per hour. How long will it take Mona to drive 100 miles? It will take Mona ________ hours to drive 100 miles.
5. The airplane flies 725 miles per hour. How many minutes will it take the plane to fly 150 miles? It will take the plane ________ minutes to fly 150 miles.	**6.** It takes Olivia 30 seconds to count to 25. How many minutes will it take Olivia to count to 300? It will take Olivia ________ minutes to count to 300.

Nonsense!

Directions: "Jabberwocky," a poem of nonsense verse, was originally featured in the book *Through the Looking Glass, and What Alice Found There* by Lewis Carroll. Read the poem, then answer the questions below.

Instrucciones: "Jabberwocky", un poema de verso sin sentido que apareció originalmente en el libro *Through the Looking Glass, and What Alice Found There* de Lewis Carroll. Lee el poema, luego contesta las siguientes preguntas.

Jabberwocky

by Lewis Carroll

'Twas brillig, and the slithy toves
Did gyre and gimble in the wabe:
All mimsy were the borogoves,
And the mome raths outgrabe.

"Beware the Jabberwock, my son!
The jaws that bite, the claws that catch!
Beware the Jubjub bird, and shun
The frumious Bandersnatch!"

He took his vorpal sword in hand:
Long time the manxome foe he sought—
So rested he by the Tumtum tree,
And stood awhile in thought.

And, as in uffish thought he stood,
The Jabberwock, with eyes of flame,
Came whiffling through the tulgey wood,
And burbled as it came!

One, two! One, two! And through and through
The vorpal blade went snicker-snack!
He left it dead, and with its head
He went galumphing back.

"And hast thou slain the Jabberwock?
Come to my arms, my beamish boy!
O frabjous day! Callooh! Callay!"
He chortled in his joy.

'Twas brillig, and the slithy toves
Did gyre and gimble in the wabe:
All mimsy were the borogoves,
And the mome raths outgrabe.

1. What did the slithy toves do in the wabe?
   - a. outgrabe
   - b. gyre and gimble
   - c. mimsy
   - d. snicker-snack

2. What is a Jabberwock?
   - a. a kind of fairy
   - b. a kind of monster
   - c. a kind of wizard
   - d. none of these

3. What kind of sound did the vorpol blade make?
   - a. burble
   - b. Callooh
   - c. snicker-snack
   - d. Callay

4. How does the poet describe the Bandersnatch?
   - a. mimsy
   - b. tulgey
   - c. uffish
   - d. frumious

Crossword Challenge

Directions: Put the words below into the crossword puzzle. Make sure that each word touches at least one other word.

Instrucciones: Coloca las siguientes palabras en el crucigrama. Asegúrate que cada palabra toque, al menos, otra palabra.

Monday Thursday Saturday

Wednesday Friday Sunday

					T	U	E	S	D	A	Y

Find the Snakes

Directions: Look for "snakes" that equal 24. The numbers have to be touching. (See the example to the right, which shows that you cannot jump around.) Once you find them, circle them. *Note:* You may use a number more than once.

Instrucciones: Busca "serpientes" que sumen 24. Los números tienen que ser conmovedores. (Ve el ejemplo a la derecha, que muestra que no puedes saltar). Una vez que los encuentres, enciérralas en un círculo. *Nota*: Puedes usar un número más de una vez.

Example:

5	+	7	+
+	8	+	12
7	+	4	+
+	9	+	6

2	+	5	×	2	+	8	×	4	÷
+	10	+	5	+	6	−	2	÷	2
5	×	3	×	2	+	6	+	5	+
×	2	+	7	+	1	×	4	×	8
3	×	12	+	2	×	2	×	3	×
+	15	−	5	÷	6	−	16	−	5
5	×	3	×	14	+	10	÷	11	−
×	6	−	1	−	6	×	4	+	4
7	−	4	+	7	+	12	+	6	×
+	11	×	2	−	16	+	15	−	4

Summer Reading List

Uno de los mejores modos de promover el desarrollo educativo durante el verano es mediante la lectura. Afortunadamente, existe una gran variedad de fantásticos libros ilustrados y de pasta dura que podrían interesas y cautivar a tu joven lector. Por favor, lee las reseñas y/o lee los libros tú mismo antes de presentárselos a tu hijo, con el fin de determinar si son adecuados para él.

Si lo deseas, puedes utilizar este gráfico (y el que figura en la páginas 93–94) para mantenerte organizado. Utiliza la columna de **Dates** para anotar el día en que tu hijo leyó el libro o cuándo debería devolverlo en la biblioteca. Utiliza la columna de **Notes** como ayuda para recordar lo que has leído en las reseñas de otros lectores o lo que tu hijo pensó del libro tras leerlo.

Dates	Book Information	Notes
	Home of the Brave by Katherine Applegate Told in verse, this is the story of a young Sudanese refugee adapting to his new life in frigid Minnesota. Throughout, he holds onto hope despite all that he has lost and forms new connections in a world that is unlike anything he has ever known. *Themes:* hope, perseverance, family, memory, culture, immigration, loss	
	Before We Were Free by Julia Alvarez Anita must hide with her family in the Dominican Republic during the 1960s. She is an average 12-year-old adolescent. She keeps a secret diary where she discusses her situation, as well as her obsession with boys and her appearance. *Themes:* family ties, courage, the cost of freedom	
	The Fighting Ground by Avi The popular children's author tells the tale of Jonathan, a 13-year-old who fights in the Revolutionary War. The boy soon finds that the real battle is within himself. *Themes:* facing fear, humanity, values	
	The Penderwicks: A Summer Tale of Four Sisters, Two Rabbits, and a Very Interesting Boy by Jeanne Birdsall Four sisters and their father spend the summer in the Berkshire Mountains. There, they share adventures with a local boy. This is a heartwarming tale of a loving family. It received the National Book Award in 2005. *Themes:* family loyalty, typical childhood behaviors, resilience	
	George Washington Carver by Tonya Bolden This is the amazing-but-true story of a man who was born a slave and became a conservationist, scientist, researcher, and teacher. It includes photos and reproductions of Carver's own paintings. *Themes:* adversity, fortitude, inventing	
	Sahara Special by Esmé Raji Codell Sahara is struggling with school and her feelings caused by her father's leaving. She gets a new start with a special teacher who supports her writing talents, as well as her individuality. *Themes:* uniqueness, inner strength, hope	
	Waiting for Normal by Leslie Connor Addie is looking for a normal life while living with her irresponsible mother in a trailer in upstate New York. This book has humor, tension, and well-developed characters. *Themes:* looking for the positive, dysfunctional parent, endurance	

Summer Reading List *(cont.)*

Dates	Book Information	Notes
	Operation Redwood by S. Terrell French Julian Carter-Li and his friends fight to save a grove of redwood trees in northern California. *Themes:* ecology, working together, fighting the establishment	
	Diamond Willow by Helen Frost Willow, a 12-year-old Alaskan girl, sets out to take her wounded dog to her grandparents' house. But during her journey, they get caught in a blizzard, and Willow must make difficult decisions. This is told in diamond-shaped, easy-to-read verse. *Themes:* connection to the past, overcoming adversity, respect for nature	
	Deep and Dark and Dangerous: A Ghost Story by Mary Downing Hahn When Ali spends the summer with her aunt and cousin at the family's vacation home, she discovers a secret her mother has been hiding for over 30 years. *Themes:* identity, overcoming fear, understanding the truth	
	Scat by Carl Hiaasen Nick and Marta must find out what happened to the biology teacher after she disappears on a school field trip to a swamp. This is an eco-mystery set in Florida. *Themes:* ecology, positive outlook, overcoming grief	
	Odysseus (retold) by Geraldine McCaughrean Odysseus journeys home after years of fighting in the Trojan War. He and his men encounter monsters, are imprisoned, and fight battles with nature as they attempt to return to Ithaca. This book is filled with violent events and gory details. *Themes:* loyalty, hardship, triumph	
	Miss Spitfire: Reaching Helen Keller by Sarah Miller This is the oft-told tale of Annie Sullivan and her challenge and determination to teach the blind and deaf Helen Keller. In this version, it is told from the point of view of Sullivan, which makes for an especially uplifting conclusion. *Themes:* never giving up, aspiration, inspiration	
	Sixth-Grade Glommers, Norks, and Me by Lisa Papademetriou This hilarious book describes Allie, who is starting middle school and is intimidated about going to a special school away from her neighborhood. *Themes:* finding your way, individualism, pride	
	A Long Walk to Water by Linda Sue Park In the 1980s, an 11-year-old Sudanese boy is forced to flee his village. His journey is filled with danger and loss, but he survives and grows up to make a difference. Around 2008, an 11-year-old Sudanese girl makes her difficult daily journey to get water for her family. Their lives connect in a hopeful and inspiring ending. *Themes:* survival, family, hope, resilience, making a difference	
	Ghost by Jason Reynolds Castle "Ghost" Cranshaw can run fast. But no one could run fast enough to escape the trauma he has endured. Ghost's anger holds him back, but a new chance emerges when the track coach takes him under his wing, showing Ghost that he is not alone and that there is a path forward. *Themes:* identity, courage, family, teamwork, mentorship, bullying	

Summer Reading List *(cont.)*

Dates	Book Information	Notes
	When You Reach Me by Rebecca Stead Miranda has her world turned upside-down when she receives some future-predicting notes. Contemporary New York City is the setting for this mystery. *Themes:* friendship, family, identity	
	The Dragonet Prophecy (Wings of Fire, Book #1) by Tui T. Sutherland Five young dragons have been secretly raised under a mountain. Each comes from a different dragon tribe, and from birth they have been told that they are destined to save Pyrrhia from the war that has erupted among the seven tribes. But with all their flaws and limitations, how can they save a world they don't even understand? The first of many books in the *Wings of Fire* series, this book does contain violence but it is very well written and beloved by those interested in dragons and epic tales. *Themes:* friendship, family, loyalty, courage, self-doubt, teamwork, growing up	
	Sisters by Raina Telgemeier Raina really wanted a younger sister, but not necessarily *this* younger sister. She and her sister seem to have so little in common except the ability to annoy each other. Taking place in the present and in numerous flashbacks, this popular graphic novel shows how two sisters are forced to bond with one another on a family road trip. *Themes:* family, connection, expectations, disappointment, shared experience	
	100 Cupboards by N. D. Wilson Twelve-year-old Henry York is sent to live with his aunt and uncle after his parents are kidnapped in South America. Soon after arriving, he finds that there is something strange in the wall behind his bed. This novel is funny, suspenseful, and gory. It is meant for the more mature reader. *Themes:* evil, overcoming obstacles, working together	

Aprovechando al máximo la lectura de verano

Cuando leas estos libros con tu hijo, puedes hacerle las preguntas que aparecen a continuación. El intercambio de preguntas, respuestas e ideas incrementará y potenciará sus habilidades de comprensión lectora. Estimúlalo a explayarse en sus respuestas y explicar sus pensamientos en detalle.

- ¿Dónde sucede el cuento? ¿Cómo es este escenario un "personaje" en el cuento?
- ¿Cuándo sucede la historia? ¿En el pasado, presente o futuro? ¿Por qué es esto importante para la trama?
- ¿Quién es un personaje principal en el cuento? ¿Cómo los eventos de la historia hacen que este personaje crezca o cambie a medida que avanza el cuento?
- Nombra un personaje secundario o sustentador ¿Por qué aparece este personaje en el cuento? Cómo ellos hacen que ocurran eventos en el cuento, y ¿cómo ayuda o perjudica esto al personaje principal?
- Nombra un conflicto en el cuento. ¿Cómo se resuelve?
- ¿Alguno de los eventos o temas de este cuento te hizo pensar en tu propia vida o examinar tu propia forma de pensar? Explicar.

Read and Do

A continuación, se incluyen algunas ideas divertidas para que tu hijo incremente su lectura. La mayoría implicarán la participación de ambos, pero se encuentran dirigidas hacia él con el fin de incentivar su amor por los libros.

Write to the Author __/__/__	Many authors love to hear from their readers, especially when they hear what people liked best about their books. You can write to an author and send your letter in care of the book's publisher. The publisher's address is listed directly after the title page. Or you may go to the author's website and follow the directions for how to send the author a letter. (To make sure your author is still living, type the author's name into a search engine.)
A Comic Book __/__/__	Turn your favorite book into a comic book. Fold at least two sheets of paper in half, and staple them so they make a book. With a ruler and pencil, draw boxes across each page to look like blank comic strips. Then, draw the story of your book as if it were a comic. Draw pictures of your characters, and have words coming out of their mouths—just as in a real comic strip.
Novel Foods __/__/__	What foods do the characters in your book eat? What do they drink? What are their favorite foods? With your parents' help, locate appropriate recipes online or in books. Make up a grocery list, buy groceries, and gather necessary materials. Cook your characters' favorite foods by yourself or with friends.
Write a Sequel __/__/__	What happens to the characters in your book after you finish reading the final page? Why not create a sequel? A sequel is a book that is published after the first book has enjoyed success among readers. Sequels generally pick up where the first book left off. For example, the sequel to Madeleine L'Engle's novel *A Wrinkle in Time* is *A Wind in the Door.*
Déjà Vu __/__/__	Did any of the events from this novel remind you of the events from a different novel or film? Write a paragraph or create a chart comparing the two pieces of art. In your opinion, which one was better? Why?
It's New to Me __/__/__	What one event from the novel's plot (or character, setting, etc.) is something you have never read about in any book before or seen in any film? Write about this element of the book and explain your thoughts about it.
If It Were Me __/__/__	Imagine that you are stuck in the world of the novel. Which event from the novel would be the most challenging (or enjoyable, frustrating, etc.) for you to deal with? Why?

Learning Experiences

A continuación, se incluyen algunas actividades divertidas y de bajo costo que puedes realizar junto a tu hijo. Pronto descubrirás que las mismas pueden ser estimulantes, educativas y complementarias del resto de los ejercicios del libro.

Tarjetas didácticas __/__/__	Elabora todo tipo de tarjetas didácticas. Dependiendo de los intereses de tu hijo y su grado académico, pueden incluir letras del abecedario, palabras de uso frecuente, o problemas matemáticos. Puedes crearlas tú mismo con marcadores o en una computadora. Sugiérele que te ayude a cortar imágenes de revistas y péguenlas en tarjetas de 3" x 5". Luego, busca un sitio al aire libre y repasen las tarjetas juntos.
Proyecto de despensa __/__/__	Encuentra un sitio en tu casa donde puedas almacenar víveres. Puede ser un armario o un contenedor que permanezca siempre en el mismo sitio. Busca algunas latas de pintura limpias o baldes. Llénalos con todo tipo de materiales para hacer manualidades. Además de las clásicas pinturas, marcadores, papel, tijeras y pegamento, puedes incluir artículos inusuales, tales como azulejos, flores artificiales y papel de regalo. De este modo, cada vez tú y tu hijo quieran hacer una manualidad, pueden acceder a todo lo necesario en ese preciso momento.
¿Cuanto cuesta? __/__/__	Si salen a comer, pide ayuda a tu hijo para obtener el total de la cuenta. Anoten el costo de la comida de cada comensal. Luego, dile que lo sume y calcule cuánto se gastó en total. Puedes modificar la actividad y volverla mucho más simple, pidiéndole que sólo calcule el costo de una entrada y un trago del menú, o el costo de tres postres. Asegúrate de redondear las cifras primero.
Búsqueda del tesoro en la naturaleza __/__/__	Salgan a caminar, vayan a un parque o realicen una excursión a las montañas. Pero antes de partir, elabora una búsqueda del tesoro para tu hijo. Puede incluir todo tipo de cosas que se puedan encontrar en la naturaleza. Asegúrate que cuente con una bolsa para guardar todo lo que encuentre (y recuerda verificar con anticipación las reglas o leyes relacionadas con la sustracción de cualquier objeto). Puedes incluir cosas tales como: una hoja con bordes puntiagudos, una roca moteada, y una ramita con dos pequeñas ramificaciones. Tómense unos minutos para observar todos los elementos que ha recolectado y táchenlos de la lista.
Realiza un viaje y lleva un diario __/__/__	Si van a realizar un viaje durante el verano, pídele a tu hijo que lleve un diario. Los niños pequeños pueden recolectar postales y pegarlas en un diario en blanco. También pueden dibujar los sitios que visitaron. Si tiene acceso a una cámara de fotos, puede armar un álbum fotográfico.

Proofreading Marks

Editor's Mark	Meaning	Example
≡	capitalize	they fished in lake tahoe.
/	make it lowercase	Five Students missed the Bus.
sp.	spelling mistake	The day was clowdy and cold.
⊙	add a period	Tomorrow is a holiday⊙
(pigtail loop)	delete (remove)	One person knew the the answer.
∧	add a word	Six pups were in the litter.
∧,	add a comma	He planted peas, corn, and squash.
∿	reverse words or letters	An otter swam in the bed kelp.
∨'	add an apostrophe	The child's bike was blue.
∨" ∨"	add quotation marks	"Why can't I go?" she cried.
#	make a space	He ate two redapples.
⁀‿	close the space	Her favorite game is soft ball.
¶	begin a new paragraph	to know. ¶Next on the list

Tough to Spell

Below and on page 99 are some of the most commonly misspelled words in the English language. Practice spelling each word, then use this list to remind you how these words are spelled.

accept ________________	grateful ________________
advice ________________	guarantee ________________
believe ________________	happily ________________
calendar ________________	harass ________________
changeable ________________	height ________________
collectible ________________	heroes ________________
congratulations ________________	humor ________________
conscience ________________	independent ________________
definitely ________________	intelligence ________________
dictionary ________________	judgment ________________
embarrass ________________	length ________________
excellence ________________	library ________________
experience ________________	lightning ________________
explanation ________________	marshmallow ________________
fascinating ________________	miniature ________________
February ________________	mischievous ________________
finally ________________	misspell ________________
foreign ________________	naturally ________________

Tough to Spell *(cont.)*

necessary ______________________

neighbor ______________________

noticeable ______________________

occasionally ______________________

opinion ______________________

opportunity ______________________

personal ______________________

piece ______________________

possession ______________________

prejudice ______________________

privilege ______________________

realize ______________________

really ______________________

receive ______________________

receipt ______________________

recommend ______________________

refrigerator ______________________

rhythm ______________________

sentence ______________________

separate ______________________

similar ______________________

success ______________________

temperature ______________________

tomorrow ______________________

truly ______________________

twelfth ______________________

unique ______________________

until ______________________

usually ______________________

vacuum ______________________

valuable ______________________

visible ______________________

weather ______________________

Wednesday ______________________

weird ______________________

writing ______________________

Multiplication Chart

×	0	1	2	3	4	5	6	7	8	9	10	11	12
0	0	0	0	0	0	0	0	0	0	0	0	0	0
1	0	1	2	3	4	5	6	7	8	9	10	11	12
2	0	2	4	6	8	10	12	14	16	18	20	22	24
3	0	3	6	9	12	15	18	21	24	27	30	33	36
4	0	4	8	12	16	20	24	28	32	36	40	44	48
5	0	5	10	15	20	25	30	35	40	45	50	55	60
6	0	6	12	18	24	30	36	42	48	54	60	66	72
7	0	7	14	21	28	35	42	49	56	63	70	77	84
8	0	8	16	24	32	40	48	56	64	72	80	88	96
9	0	9	18	27	36	45	54	63	72	81	90	99	108
10	0	10	20	30	40	50	60	70	80	90	100	110	120
11	0	11	22	33	44	55	66	77	88	99	110	121	132
12	0	12	24	36	48	60	72	84	96	108	120	132	144

Division Tables

Divided by 1
1 ÷ 1 = 1
2 ÷ 1 = 2
3 ÷ 1 = 3
4 ÷ 1 = 4
5 ÷ 1 = 5
6 ÷ 1 = 6
7 ÷ 1 = 7
8 ÷ 1 = 8
9 ÷ 1 = 9
10 ÷ 1 = 10
11 ÷ 1 = 11
12 ÷ 1 = 12

Divided by 2
2 ÷ 2 = 1
4 ÷ 2 = 2
6 ÷ 2 = 3
8 ÷ 2 = 4
10 ÷ 2 = 5
12 ÷ 2 = 6
14 ÷ 2 = 7
16 ÷ 2 = 8
18 ÷ 2 = 9
20 ÷ 2 = 10
22 ÷ 2 = 11
24 ÷ 2 = 12

Divided by 3
3 ÷ 3 = 1
6 ÷ 3 = 2
9 ÷ 3 = 3
12 ÷ 3 = 4
15 ÷ 3 = 5
18 ÷ 3 = 6
21 ÷ 3 = 7
24 ÷ 3 = 8
27 ÷ 3 = 9
30 ÷ 3 = 10
33 ÷ 3 = 11
36 ÷ 3 = 12

Divided by 4
4 ÷ 4 = 1
8 ÷ 4 = 2
12 ÷ 4 = 3
16 ÷ 4 = 4
20 ÷ 4 = 5
24 ÷ 4 = 6
28 ÷ 4 = 7
32 ÷ 4 = 8
36 ÷ 4 = 9
40 ÷ 4 = 10
44 ÷ 4 = 11
48 ÷ 4 = 12

Divided by 5
5 ÷ 5 = 1
10 ÷ 5 = 2
15 ÷ 5 = 3
20 ÷ 5 = 4
25 ÷ 5 = 5
30 ÷ 5 = 6
35 ÷ 5 = 7
40 ÷ 5 = 8
45 ÷ 5 = 9
50 ÷ 5 = 10
55 ÷ 5 = 11
60 ÷ 5 = 12

Divided by 6
6 ÷ 6 = 1
12 ÷ 6 = 2
18 ÷ 6 = 3
24 ÷ 6 = 4
30 ÷ 6 = 5
36 ÷ 6 = 6
42 ÷ 6 = 7
48 ÷ 6 = 8
54 ÷ 6 = 9
60 ÷ 6 = 10
66 ÷ 6 = 11
72 ÷ 6 = 12

Divided by 7
7 ÷ 7 = 1
14 ÷ 7 = 2
21 ÷ 7 = 3
28 ÷ 7 = 4
35 ÷ 7 = 5
42 ÷ 7 = 6
49 ÷ 7 = 7
56 ÷ 7 = 8
63 ÷ 7 = 9
70 ÷ 7 = 10
77 ÷ 7 = 11
84 ÷ 7 = 12

Divided by 8
8 ÷ 8 = 1
16 ÷ 8 = 2
24 ÷ 8 = 3
32 ÷ 8 = 4
40 ÷ 8 = 5
48 ÷ 8 = 6
56 ÷ 8 = 7
64 ÷ 8 = 8
72 ÷ 8 = 9
80 ÷ 8 = 10
88 ÷ 8 = 11
96 ÷ 8 = 12

Divided by 9
9 ÷ 9 = 1
18 ÷ 9 = 2
27 ÷ 9 = 3
36 ÷ 9 = 4
45 ÷ 9 = 5
54 ÷ 9 = 6
63 ÷ 9 = 7
72 ÷ 9 = 8
81 ÷ 9 = 9
90 ÷ 9 = 10
99 ÷ 9 = 11
108 ÷ 9 = 12

Divided by 10
10 ÷ 10 = 1
20 ÷ 10 = 2
30 ÷ 10 = 3
40 ÷ 10 = 4
50 ÷ 10 = 5
60 ÷ 10 = 6
70 ÷ 10 = 7
80 ÷ 10 = 8
90 ÷ 10 = 9
100 ÷ 10 = 10
110 ÷ 10 = 11
120 ÷ 10 = 12

Divided by 11
11 ÷ 11 = 1
22 ÷ 11 = 2
33 ÷ 11 = 3
44 ÷ 11 = 4
55 ÷ 11 = 5
66 ÷ 11 = 6
77 ÷ 11 = 7
88 ÷ 11 = 8
99 ÷ 11 = 9
110 ÷ 11 = 10
121 ÷ 11 = 11
132 ÷ 11 = 12

Divided by 12
12 ÷ 12 = 1
24 ÷ 12 = 2
36 ÷ 12 = 3
48 ÷ 12 = 4
60 ÷ 12 = 5
72 ÷ 12 = 6
84 ÷ 12 = 7
96 ÷ 12 = 8
108 ÷ 12 = 9
120 ÷ 12 = 10
132 ÷ 12 = 11
144 ÷ 12 = 12

Area and Volume

Area Formulas

Square

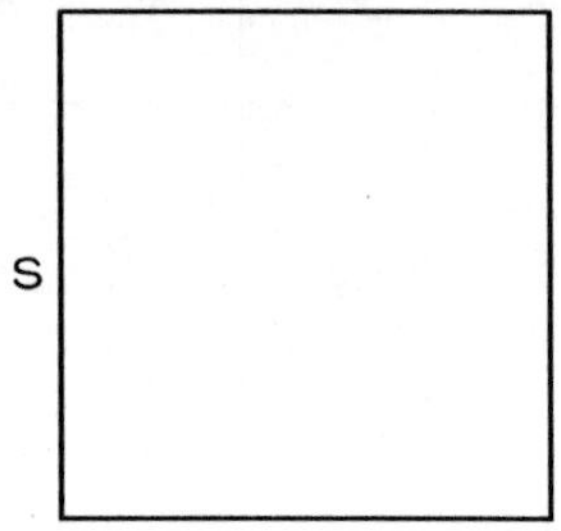

$A = s^2$

Rectangle

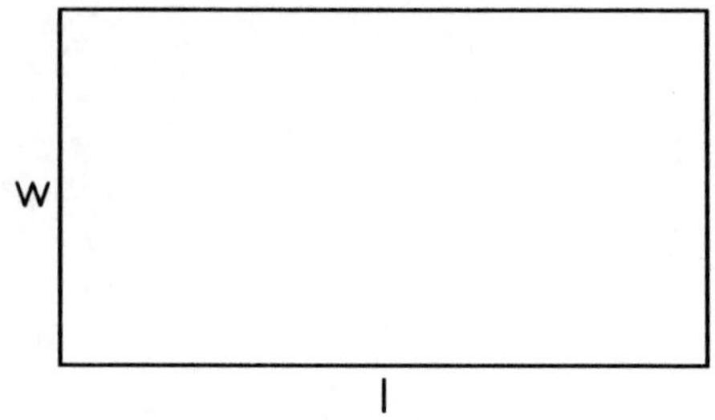

$A = l \times w$

Triangle

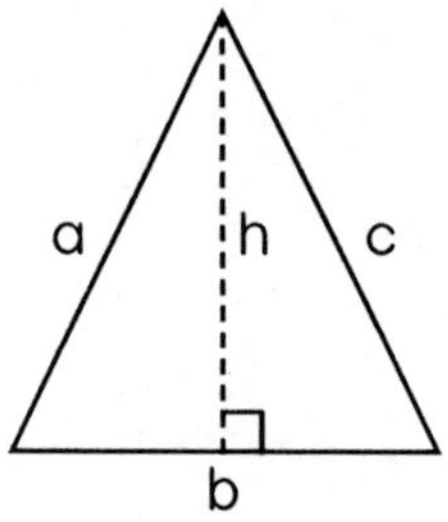

$A = \frac{1}{2} bh$

Volume Formulas

Cube

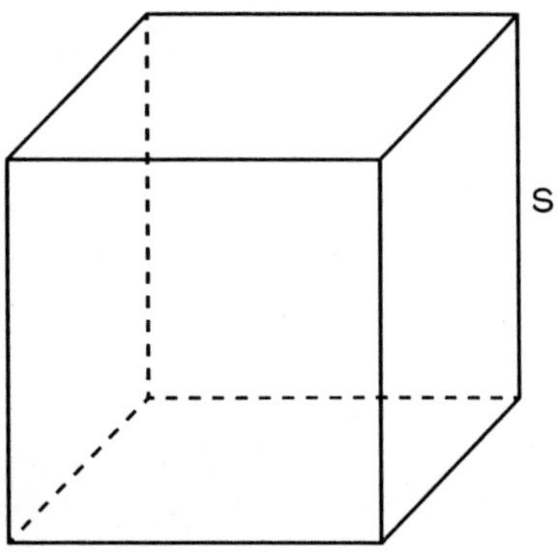

$V = s^3$

Rectangular Prism

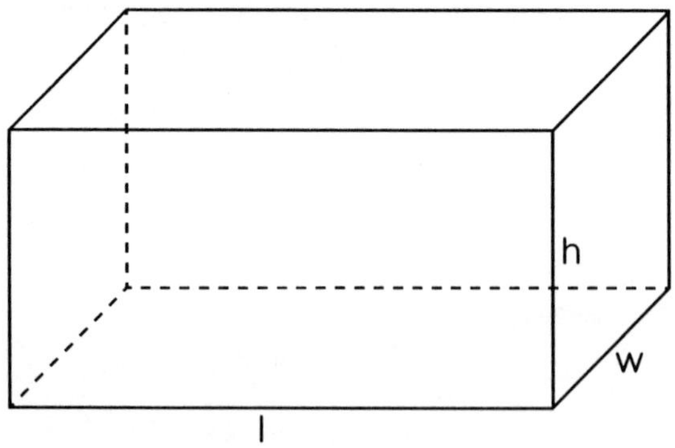

$V = l \times w \times h$

Fraction Math

Adding Fractions

If two fractions have the same denominator (bottom number), then simply add the two numerators (top numbers) together. The denominator stays the same.

Add the numerators. → *Do not add the denominators.* →

$$\frac{1}{4} + \frac{2}{4} = \frac{3}{4}$$

If two fractions have different denominators, then convert one or both of the fractions so that until they have the lowest common denominator possible.

$$\frac{1}{4} + \frac{4}{6} = \frac{3}{12} + \frac{8}{12} = \frac{11}{12}$$

12 is the lowest common denominator.

Subtracting Fractions

This works in the same way as adding fractions. If the denominators are the same, simply subtract the numerators.

$$\frac{1}{4} - \frac{1}{10} = \frac{5}{20} - \frac{2}{20} = \frac{3}{20}$$

If the denominators are different, then first find the lowest common denominator before subtracting the numerators.

Multiplying Fractions

When multiplying fractions, simply multiply across. This means that the numerators of the fractions are multiplied together to find the new numerator. And the denominators of the fractions are multiplied together to find the new denominator.

$$\frac{2}{3} \times \frac{3}{5} = \frac{6}{15} = \frac{2}{5}$$

← *If the answer can be simplified, then do that.*

Dividing Fractions

Dividing fractions is similar to multiplying them, except with a little twist. Take the divisor (the fraction after the division sign) and flip it. Then multiply the two fractions.

$$\frac{1}{2} \div \frac{1}{3} = \frac{1}{2} \times \frac{3}{1} = \frac{3}{2} = 1\frac{1}{2}$$

← *If possible, convert the answer (quotient) to lowest terms.*

Answer Key

Page 12

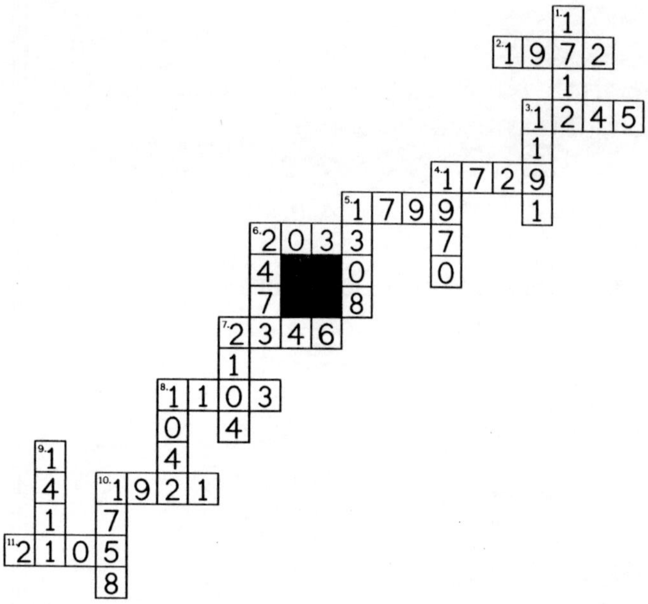

Page 13

1. b 2. b 3. c 4. a

Page 14

2. 1,836
3. 1,207
4. 77,924
5. 32,824
6. 32,103
7. 8,475
8. 109,272
9. 992,200
10. 43,183
11. 19,783
12. 98,256

Page 16

2. 41,792 ÷ 172 = 243
   Check: 243 × 172 = 41,796
3. 33,320 ÷ 136 = 245
   Check: 245 × 136 = 33,320
4. 3,822 ÷ 91 = 42
   Check: 42 × 91 = 3,822
5. 8,928 ÷ 9 = 992
   Check: 992 × 9 = 8,928
6. 28,917 ÷ 81 = 357
   Check: 357 × 81 = 28,917
7. 35,620 ÷ 260 = 137
   Check: 137 × 260 = 35,620
8. 180,930 ÷ 37 = 4,890
   Check: 4,890 × 37 = 180,930
9. 8,840 ÷ 65 = 136
   Check: 136 × 65 = 8,840

Page 17

1. a 2. b 3. d 4. a

Page 18

1. $89.76
2. $13.47
3. $105.30
4. $139.93
5. $53.38
6. $420.52
7. $481.39
8. $256.50
9. 2.646
10. 1.872
11. 2.6628
12. 0.00228
13. $6.30
14. 4.78
15. 137.74

Page 19

2. B, antonyms
3. C, antonyms
4. D, synonyms
5. B, antonyms
6. B, synonyms
7. C, synonyms
8. A, antonyms
9. A, synonyms

Page 20

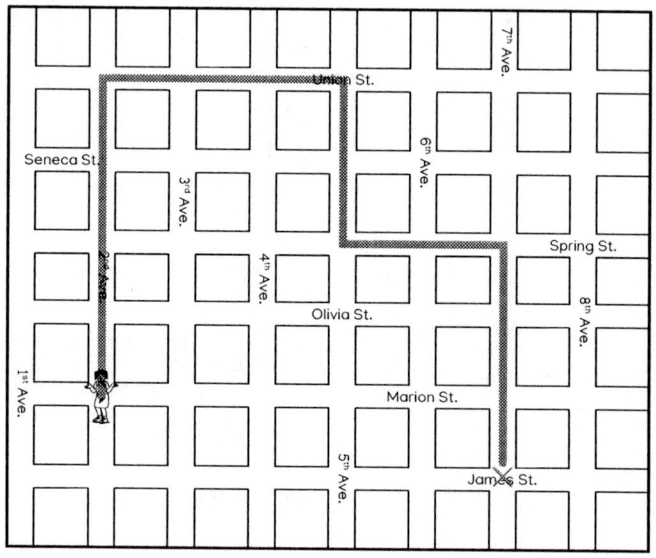

Page 21

2. caribou
3. okapi
4. llama
5. oyster
6. eagle
7. ferret
8. jaguar
9. manatee
10. cobra

Answer Key *(cont.)*

Page 22

Page 23

Page 24

1. 15 minutes/900 seconds
2. 30 minutes/1,800 seconds
3. 45 minutes/2,700 seconds
4. 60 minutes/3,600 seconds
5. 120 minutes/7,200 seconds
6. 180 minutes/10,800 seconds
7. 240 minutes/14,400 seconds
8. 360 minutes/21,600 seconds
9. 480 minutes/28,800 seconds
10. 720 minutes/43,200 seconds
11. 1,080 minutes/64,800 seconds
12. 1,440 minutes/86,400 seconds

13. > 14. < 15. > 16. <

Page 25

1. a 2. c 3. b 4. c

Page 26

1. 5	4. 750	7. 275.88
2. 72	5. 175	8. 2.67
3. 25	6. 81.25	9. 0.04

Page 27

Answers will vary, but words may be used in the following ways:

1. Avery's *fast* lasted six days. (n)
   Joey ran very *fast*. (adv)
2. Corinne stood by her friend's *side*. (n)
   The thief left using the *side* door. (adv)
3. Which *number* did you draw? (n)
   Number your paper one through six. (v)
4. Get a *good* night's sleep before the test. (adj)
   The peddler sold his *goods* from a truck. (n)
5. Our lawyer thinks we have a *just* cause. (adj)
   That cake has *just* enough chocolate in it. (adv)
6. Our captain ordered a *retreat* from the field. (n)
   "*Retreat!*" yelled our captain. (v)

Answer Key *(cont.)*

Page 28

1. 467.476 mi.
2. 2,246.8 mi.
3. 32.422 ft.
4. 94.14 mi.
5. 23.23 mi.
6. 44.636 mi.
7. 47.813 m.p.h.
8. 3,030.957 lbs.
9. 91.05 mi.
10. 880.431 mi.

Page 29

1. a **2.** c **3.** b **4.** c

Page 30

1. puppy: 94, kitten: 79
2. igloo: 58, house: 68
3. pizza: 78, sandwich: 81

Page 31

1. Nets
2. Padres
3. Dolphins
4. Colts
5. Eagles
6. Lions
7. Pistons
8. Marlins
9. Jazz
10. Kings
11. Clippers
12. Broncos
13. Diamondbacks
14. Lightning

Page 32

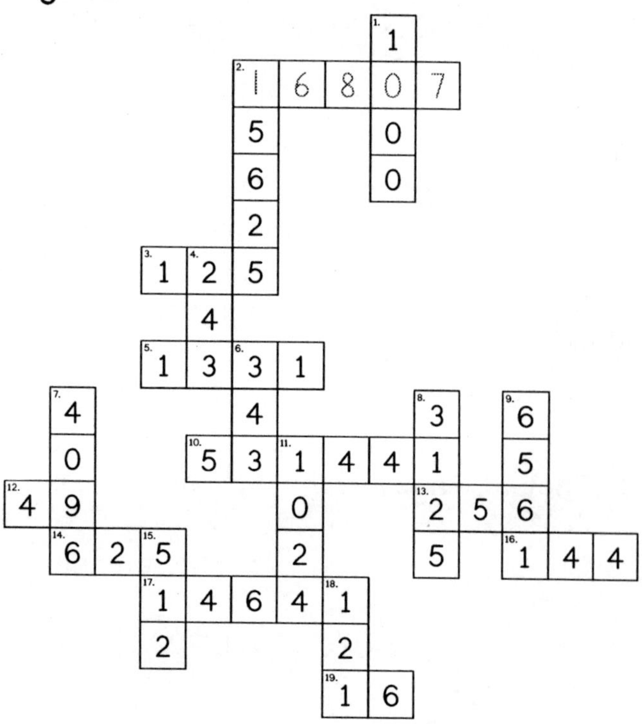

Page 33

The main idea is *b*.

1. A great monster leaped from the shadows and blocked their way.
2. The ugly beast had purple eyes.
3. Above them, a horn rose from the center of its forehead.
4. Its bright orange skin showed beneath a thin layer of coarse, black hair.
5. It reached its claws toward the terrified group.
6. It snarled menacingly, revealing a mouthful of sharp teeth.

Page 34

H. 2	**W.** –15	**E.** –16	**I.** –5
Q. –4	**K.** –6	**Y.** 5	**P.** 22
D. –2	**X.** –21	**J.** –21	**T.** 3
B. –18	**S.** –1	**Z.** 8	**R.** –20
F. 0	**A.** –9	**C.** 13	**L.** –41
G. –11	**V.** 6	**N.** 1	
O. –3	**U.** 11	**M.** 12	

Riddle: Eleven: three in "the" and eight in "alphabet"

Page 36

1. $1	**4.** 7	**7.** $6	**10.** –72
2. $1	**5.** $21	**8.** –24	**11.** –32
3. $11	**6.** 2	**9.** 17	**12.** $226

Page 37

1. ABN
2. 1 hour
3. no
4. ABN
5. repeat
6. 3
7. *Night Train*, *Stage Divers*, or Movie: *Ozone*
8. False
9. False
10. True
11. Saturday, January 22
12. *Holiday Line*

Answer Key *(cont.)*

Page 38

1. \$12
2. \$20
3. 42
4. \$7
5. –9
6. 10
7. \$270
8. 156
9. –64
10. 5
11. \$5
12. 20

Page 40

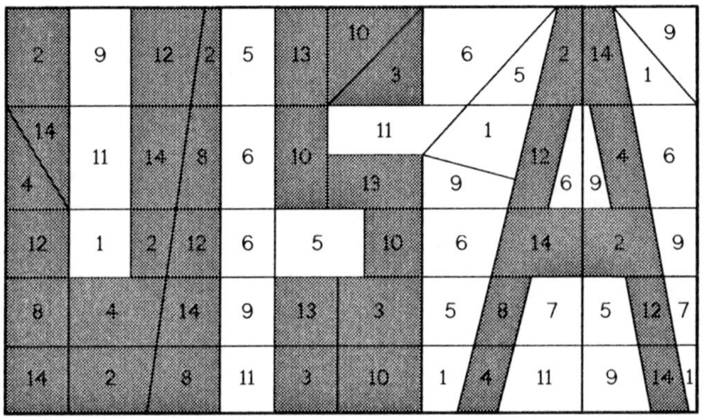

Page 41

1. Patriots
2. Twins
3. Timberwolves
4. Avalanche
5. Rockets
6. Dodgers
7. Sharks
8. Bucks
9. Bulls
10. A's
11. 49ers
12. Heat, Suns

Page 42

2. 30
3. 25
4. 1
5. 63
6. 53
7. 6
8. 18
9. 38
10. 20
11. 86
12. 36
13. 8
14. 5
15. 18

Page 44

1. 130 yds.
2. 240 cm
3. 340 ft.
4. 630 m
5. 238 cm
6. 722 mm
7. 221 m
8. 85.8 cm

Page 45

1. c
2. a
3. a

Page 46

1. 240
2. 450
3. 1,035
4. 240
5. 4,171
6. 1,155
7. 672
8. 87.5
9. 99.6
10. 484

Page 47

1. flew
2. swam
3. cried
4. drank
5. went
6. sped
7. ran
8. sang
9. drew
10. ate
11. bought
12. spoke
13. rode
14. wore
15. grew
16. froze
17. made
18. slept

Answers will vary. Possible answers:

19. went
20. am
21. threw
22. groans
23. hides
24. are going
25. will live
26. earned

Page 48

1. $7 \times 5 \times 7 = 245$ cubic units
2. $6 \times 4 \times 5 = 120$ cubic units
3. $3 \times 1 \times 6 = 18$ cubic units
4. $1^3 = 1$ cubic unit
5. $7^3 = 343$ cubic units
6. $5^3 = 125$ cubic units

Page 49

1. irrigate
2. exaggerate
3. accumulate
4. calculate
5. contribute
6. substitute
7. anticipate
8. retrieve
9. contribute
10. retrieve
11. exaggerate
12. calculate
13. accumulate
14. substitute
15. anticipate
16. irrigate

Answer Key *(cont.)*

Page 50

2. eight
3. bawl
4. choose
5. course
6. daze
7. dear
8. hair
9. whole
10. gene
11. least
12. maid
13. mane
14. knight
15. pause
16. read
17. seen
18. steak
19. steel
20. straight

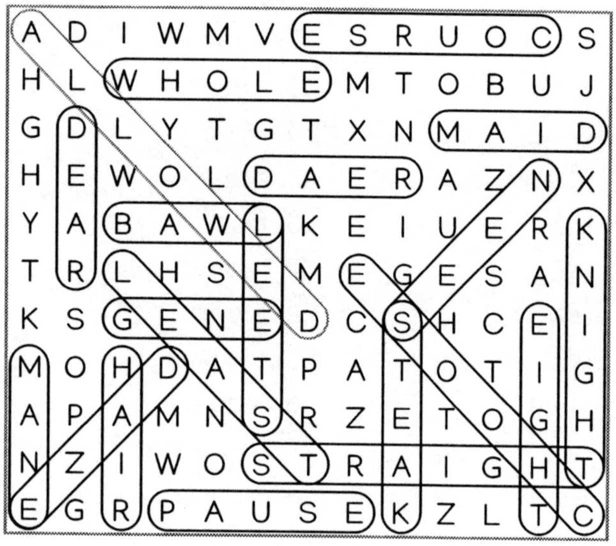

Page 51

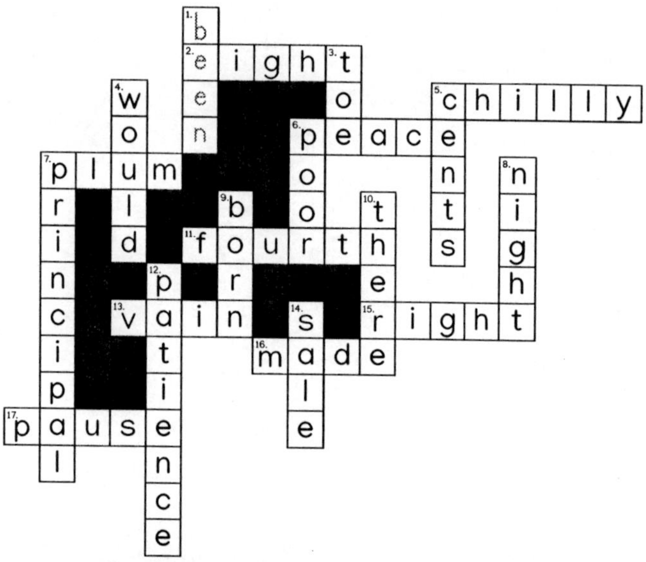

Page 52

1. b **2.** b **3.** d **4.** c **5.** d **6.** a **7.** c **8.** d **9.** c **10.** b

Page 53

1. d **2.** b **3.** a **4.** c

Page 54

steal its chair

Page 55

1. subject
2. subject
3. subject
4. verb
5. verb
6. verb

Page 56

1. (11, 5)
2. (3, 0)
3. (6, 1)
4. (12, 12)
5. (4, 4)
6. (10, 8)
7. (8, 6)
8. (2, 11)
9. (6, 10)
10. (3, 7)
11. (1, 3)
12. (10, 2)

Page 57

1. c **2.** b **3.** True

Page 58

1. $\frac{11}{14}$
2. $1\frac{13}{18}$
3. $\frac{14}{19}$
4. $\frac{82}{87}$
5. $\frac{18}{29}$
6. $1\frac{1}{4}$
7. $\frac{2}{3}$
8. 5
9. $\frac{3}{4}$
10. $\frac{3}{4}$
11. $2\frac{1}{6}$
12. $\frac{3}{7}$
13. $1\frac{1}{9}$
14. $\frac{8}{9}$
15. $1\frac{5}{27}$
16. $\frac{3}{10}$
17. $3\frac{1}{9}$
18. $6\frac{1}{4}$
19. $9\frac{3}{4}$
20. $\frac{1}{4}$
21. $\frac{25}{133}$
22. $\frac{5}{64}$
23. $2\frac{31}{32}$
24. $33\frac{3}{4}$

Page 60

Matt lives in apartment number 212.
Brandon lives in apartment number 213.
Gary lives in apartment number 210.
Louisa lives in apartment number 214.
Maria lives in apartment number 215.
Violet lives in apartment number 211.

Answer Key *(cont.)*

Page 61

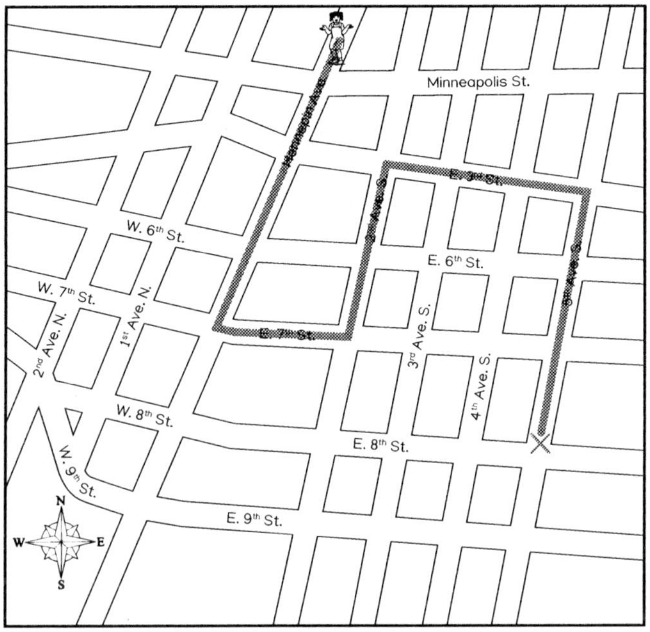

Page 62

1. c **3.** d **5.** c **7.** a

2. b **4.** d **6.** a **8.** c

Page 64

1. $\frac{7}{12}$ lb.

2. $1\frac{5}{12}$ lbs.

3. $\frac{1}{8}$ lb.

4. $\frac{1}{12}$ lb.

5. 5 lbs.

6. $\frac{1}{4}$ ft.

7. $1\frac{7}{10}$ lbs.

8. $\frac{11}{24}$ ft.

9. 6 cups

10. $1\frac{19}{30}$ lb.

Page 65

1. a **2.** b, d

Page 66

1. c

2. d

3. b, 200 words times 8% frequency = 16

4. e, i, n, l, c, p

5. a: 25%, b: 25%, e: 12.5%, l: 25%, s: 12.5%

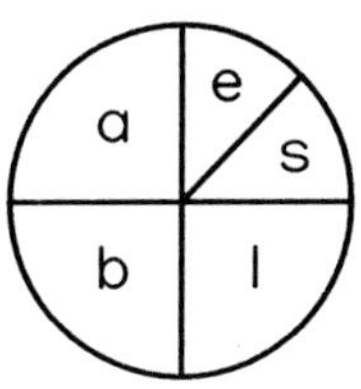

The order of the letters may vary.

Page 67

Answers will vary, but check for appropriate punctuation and conjunctions.

Page 68

Part I

1. \$42.29 **2.** c **3.** \$1,372.70

Part II

1. $\frac{1}{10}$, .10, 10%

2. $\frac{1}{4}$, .25, 25%

3. $\frac{9}{20}$, .45, 45%

4. $\frac{3}{20}$, .15, 15%

5. $\frac{4}{5}$, .80, 80%

Page 69

Part I

My favorite poem, "Love Is Alive," was written by American poet Sophie Harrington. I read anything written by or about her that I can find. I was especially happy to find that, in my subscription to *Grandeur*, there was an article entitled "Up and Coming Poets" that featured Sophie and her work. As I read the article, I was surprised to discover that she has also written several short stories. Her latest short story, "The How and Why of It All," is scheduled to be in the next issue of *Grandeur*. Since I too am a writer, she has inspired me to begin writing a song that I've tentatively titled, "My Inspiration." I may even send her a copy of it, once I have it completed.

Page 70

1. foreign language

2. hanging around

3. I'm on your side.

4. paradise

5. checkup

6. domino

7. Go for it.

8. sitting on top of the world

9. one in a million

Answer Key *(cont.)*

Page 71

2. egg
3. cream
4. bag
5. light
6. apple
7. pen
8. horse
9. eye
10. pack
11. fire
12. air

Page 72

1. 54
2. 40
3. 4
4. 16
5. 4
6. New York
7. 254
8. 284
9. There are more electoral votes in Florida.
10. 16

Page 73

1. c
2. a
3. b
4. a
5. b
6. c
7. c
8. b

Page 74

1. 30%
2. 5th and 8th
3. 60%
4. about 45%
5. 40%

Page 75

1. at the South Pole
2. during the speech
3. in the pan
4. on TV
5. under the table
6. to the movies
7. across the road
8. to the top

Page 76

1. total: 528; divided by: 9; average: 58.67
2. total: 911; divided by: 11; average: 82.82
3. total: 1,160; divided by: 13; average: 89.23
4. total: 138; divided by: 10; average: 13.8
5. total: 175; divided by: 13; average: 13.46
6. total: 107; divided by: 16; average: 6.69

Page 77

1. c
2. c
3. Michael and Cheryl did not get along very well. They both did things to upset the other.
4. Answers will vary.
5. b

Page 78

1. 37
2. 38.5
3. 42

Page 80

	5:45	6:00	6:15	6:30	6:45	Dessert	Rolls	Salad	Sodas	Spaghetti
Betty	X	X	O	X	X	X	X	X	X	O
Charice	X	O	X	X	X	X	O	X	X	X
Heidi	X	X	X	O	X	X	X	O	X	X
Paul	O	X	X	X	X	O	X	X	X	X
Roland	X	X	X	X	O	X	X	X	O	X

1. Betty arrived at **6:15** and brought the **spaghetti.**
2. Charice arrived at **6:00** and brought the **rolls.**
3. Heidi arrived at **6:30** and brought the **salad.**
4. Paul arrived at **5:45** and brought the **dessert.**
5. Roland arrived at **6:45** and brought the **sodas.**

Page 82

1. 2
2. 4
3. 7
4. 9
5. 10
6. 8
7. 11
8. 12
9. 13
10. 15
11. 14
12. 20
13. 30
14. 70
15. 80
16. 40
17. 700
18. 800
19. 400
20. 900
21. 500
22. 300
23. 600
24. 100

Answer Key *(cont.)*

Page 83

1. Zeus asked Echo to distract his wife, Hera, by talking to her.
2. Zeus asked Echo to do this so that Hera wouldn't notice that he was with other women.
3. Hera figured out what Zeus and Echo were up to and became furious. She took away Echo's ability to speak normally; Echo could only repeat the last word spoken to her.
4. Echo fell in love with Narcissus because he was so handsome.
5. Narcissus rejected Echo.
6. Nemesis punished Narcissus by making him fall in love with his own reflection.
7. Echo hid in a cave and wasted away until all that remained of her was her ability to repeat the last word spoken to her.
8. Unable to move away from his beautiful reflection, Narcissus wasted away at the edge of the pool until he vanished. A yellow flower grew in the place where he had sat.

Page 84

2. 4:5 or 4/5
3. 2:5 or 2/5
4. 5:2 or 5/2
5. 3:5 or 3/5
6. 5:3 or 5/3
7. 4:3 or 4/3
8. 3:4 or 3/4
9. 2:3 or 2/3
10. 3:2 or 3/2
11. 7:5 or 7/5
12. 5:7 or 5/7
13. 3:7 or 3/7
14. 7:3 or 7/3

Page 85

1. b 2. a 3. c 4. a 5. c

Page 86

1. 60
2. 50
3. 30
4. 60
5. 50
6. 55
7. 51
8. 40
9. 40
10. 130

Page 88

2. 5
3. 8
4. 2.5
5. 12.41
6. 6

Page 89

1. b 2. b 3. c 4. d

Page 90

Answers will vary but may include:

									T		F
							W		H		R
							E		U		I
							D		R		D
							N		S		A
	S				T	U	E	S	D	A	Y
	U						S		A		
	N			M	O	N	D	A	Y		
	D						A				
S	A	T	U	R	D	A	Y				
	Y										

Page 91

2	+	5	×	2	+	8	×	4	÷
+	10	+	5	+	6	−	2	÷	2
5	×	3	×	2	+	6	+	5	+
×	2	+	7	+	1	×	4	×	8
3	×	12	+	2	×	2	×	3	×
+	15	−	5	÷	6	−	16	−	5
5	×	3	×	14	+	10	÷	11	−
×	6	−	1	−	6	×	4	+	4
7	−	4	+	7	+	12	+	6	×
+	11	×	2	−	16	+	15	−	4

Reward Chart